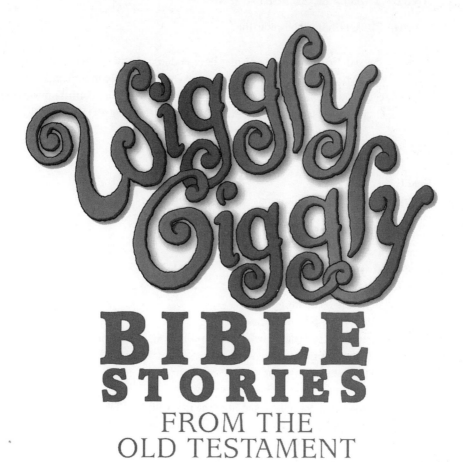

BIBLE
STORIES
FROM THE
OLD TESTAMENT

Group
Loveland, Colorado

Wiggly, Giggly Bible Stories From The Old Testament

Copyright © 2000 Group Publishing, Inc.

Visit our Web site: **www.grouppublishing.com**

Credits
Contributing Authors: Jody Brolsma, Laurie Casteñeda, Cindy Kenney, Jan Kershner, Julie Lavender, Carol Mader, and Barbie Murphy
Editor: Linda A. Anderson
Creative Development Editor: Jim Kochenburger
Chief Creative Officer: Joani Schultz
Copy Editor: Dena Twinem
Art Director: Jenette McEntire
Designers: Kari K. Monson and Jenette McEntire
Computer Graphic Artists: Nighthawk Design and Tracy K. Donaldson
Illustrator: Michael Morris
Production Manager: Peggy Naylor

Library of Congress Cataloging-in-Publication Data

Wiggly, giggly Bible stories from the Old Testament.
    p. cm.
  Includes index.
  ISBN 0-7644-2145-X (alk. paper)
   1. Christian education of preschool children. 2. Bible. O.T.--Biography--Study and teaching (Early childhood)--Activity programs. I. Group Publishing.

  BV1475.7 .W542 2000
  221.9'505--dc21

                                                     99-045914

10 9 8 7 6 5 4 3 2   09 08 07 06 05 04 03 02 01 00
Printed in the United States of America.

Contents

Introduction

Preschoolers crave age-appropriate and action-packed activities that match their short attention spans. They respond with delight to stories that appeal to their five senses and various learning styles. They're also excited about action heroes. *Wiggly, Giggly Bible Stories From the Old Testament* will help you give your preschoolers what they need and want. This is a collection of action-packed stories about twenty-five Old Testament heroes. Each story is told in at least four fun and very active ways—ways that will have your children moving, singing, laughing, and learning.

We selected twenty-five Bible heroes—both men and women—from the Old Testament. Their stories are explored through motion songs, finger plays, easy dramas, quick crafts, and edible crafts. Children will meet men and women who learned the importance of obedience to God and the rewards of bravery. They will even learn that God has big plans for little people like them.

This book is super for those times when children are too wiggly and giggly to sit still during the Bible story. You'll also find that it's just what you need when you're teaching an extended session and need a fresh way to tell or review the story. No matter how large or small your class may be, all of the children in your class will be actively involved in creative learning activities.

Enjoy using the stories in *Wiggly, Giggly Bible Stories From the Old Testament* to introduce the children in your class to the great heroes of the Old Testament. You'll find that children love actively exploring their favorite Bible stories as well as stories that are brand-new to them. They'll want to hear and tell these stories again and again. And you'll love the learning that comes when excited children have fun with Bible stories.

What better reward can you have than to see your preschoolers really learning God's Word? These memorable stories will keep them coming back for more. And you'll discover that the anticipation and excitement are not theirs alone. You'll be coming back for more too! So come along and experience the joy of fun-filled learning!

Noah
Genesis 6–9

The story of Noah is an enjoyable tale that will help little ones learn about one man who became a hero because of his obedience to God. Noah's belief and trust in God sustained him as he prepared for impending disaster. Through this story, little ones can learn to listen, obey, and trust even when God doesn't seem to make sense.

Noah Listened to God!

Children will enjoy this action rhyme as they learn how Noah listened to God. Say each verse while demonstrating the actions that accompany it.

Noah was a faithful man who listened to what God said. *(Cup hand to ear.)*

Not like the others who pushed God away and did what they wanted instead. *(Push hands away from body, and then put them on hips.)*

So God said to Noah, "Please listen to me, this is what you should do. *(Cup hand to ear and hold one finger up.)*

Build me an ark, make it really big, because the sky will no longer be blue! *(Pretend to hammer, and then stretch arms wide.)*

It's going to rain for a really long time, and I want you to be ready." *(Twinkle fingers from high to low to look like rain.)*

So Noah built that ark as big as God said; he worked long and steady. *(Pretend to hammer, then cup hand over eyes and look out.)*

Then God said to Noah, "See? I am sending the animals two by two. *(Point away from body, then hold up two fingers, two times.)*

Bring them on board with your family, this is what I want you to do." *(Wave hand in toward body.)*

Then it started to rain for forty days and nights, and the water rose up to
their heads! *(Twinkle fingers high to low to look like rain, then show a high
level of rain by stretching out one hand high.)*

Because God was angry at those who pushed him away and did what *they*
wanted instead. *(Make an angry face and push hands away from body.)*

When the rain finally stopped, Noah sent out a dove to see if the dove
could find land. *(Flap arms like a bird.)*

And the bird soon came back with a twig in its beak which he laid right
in Noah's hand. *(Flap arms, then hold out hand.)*

The water had dried up, and up in the sky was such a beautiful sight!
(Spread arms out to show God's beauty.)

A rainbow from God, a promise he made, to never cause us such a fright!
(Make a wide arc with hands in the air.)

Two by Two

This song will help kids remember Noah's obedience and faith in God. Sing it to
the tune of "Row, Row, Row Your Boat." The actions will add fun for children.

Build, build, build an ark. *(Hammer with one fist into other open hand.)*
That's what Noah did! *(Continue hammering.)*
God told him to build the ark. *(Point up with one hand.)*
So that's what Noah did. *(Fold arms over chest and nod head "yes.")*

Two, two, two by two *(hold up two fingers on one hand and wave back and
forth)*
Animals in the ark! *(Jump up and down.)*
Two of every single kind *(hold up two fingers again)*
Of animals in the ark! *(Jump up and down again.)*

Rain, rain, rain, and more *(spread out fingers on both hands high over head, and
then wiggle them as you move arms down)*
Forty days and nights! *(Hold hands up with fingers spread wide apart for "days,"
and then close fingers into a fist for "nights.")*
Filled the earth and floated the ark *(move arms in a wide circle)*
For forty days and nights. *(Hold hands up with fingers spread wide apart for
"days," and then close fingers into a fist for "nights.")*

Look, look, look in the sky. *(Put hand over eyes and look up.)*
See what God has done! *(Point up with one hand.)*

He put a rainbow in the sky. *(Move one arm in an arc over head.)*
That's what God has done! *(Point up with one hand.)*

Noah's Animal Dance

Really get out those wiggles and giggles as preschoolers learn about Noah and do this animal dance! Teach children the words, then dance the way the animals dance!

Verse 1: **God told Noah to build an ark.** *(Pretend to build.)*
It was so big it filled a park! *(Spread arms wide.)*
It rained for forty nights and days *(hold hands up with fingers spread wide apart for "days," and then close fingers into a fist for "nights")*
For people did not follow God's ways! *(Fold arms over chest and shake head "no.")*
Come on, let's dance like the animals do!
Come on, let's dance like a kangaroo!

Verse 2: **When the rain was done and the sun came out** *(spread arms and fingers)*
The dove came back, there can be no doubt! *(Shake head "no.")*
The colors in the sky were as pretty as can be *(twinkle fingers in the air)*
'Cause God sent a rainbow just for you and me! *(Make an arc in the air.)*
Come on, let's dance with the colors in the sky!
Come on, let's dance like a butterfly!

Repeat verse 1, but use the following as the last two lines:
Come on, let's dance, don't save it for later!
Come on, let's dance like an alligator!

Repeat verse 2, but use the following as the last two lines:
Come on, let's dance, we're gonna get funky!
Come on, let's dance just like a monkey!

Repeat verse 1, but use the following as the last two lines:
Come on, let's dance, let's do it with flair!
Come on, let's dance just like a bear!

Repeat verse 2, but use the following as the last two lines:
Come on, let's dance and do some kickin'!
Come on, let's dance just like a chicken!

Noah's Rainbow

Kids will enjoy making rainbows to help them remember the story of Noah. Give each child half of a white paper plate. Each child will also need the following colors of crayons: red, orange, yellow, green, blue, dark blue, and purple.

Let kids create rainbows using each color the way they want as you explain what that color represents.

The color red reminds me of God's sadness in the people. That's why God made it rain.

The color orange is for the animals that God sent, two by two, onto the ark. He brought birds, snakes, furry animals, and insects!

The color yellow makes me think of the sun that was blocked out by the rain, but then began to shine again after forty days and nights.

The color green reminds me of the earth that disappeared when it rained for such a long time! It also stands for the olive branch the dove brought back in its mouth to show that the dry land had reappeared again after the rain.

The color blue is for Noah's faith that helped him work so long to build the ark. Noah was true-blue!

Dark blue looks like the water that got higher and higher as it rained for forty days and nights.

The color purple is for the rainbow that God put up in the sky to promise us that he will never make it rain like that again.

Noah in the Ark

This quick and active game will have all the children involved in the story of Noah and the animals on the ark. Teach the children words to this song sung to the tune of "The Farmer in the Dell." Start with one child in the middle as Noah and have the rest of the children form a circle around "Noah" and sing the song. "Noah" will choose another child to join him or her at the end of the first verse and that child will choose then next and so forth. Add as many kinds of animals as you need until all the children have been selected, and then end with the final verse.

Noah in the ark,
Noah in the ark,
God had a plan to save
Noah in the ark.

Noah picks a wife,
Noah picks a wife.
To sail along inside the ark,
Noah picks a wife.

His wife picks a son,
His wife picks a son.
To sail along inside the ark,
His wife picks a son.

The son picks a wife,
The son picks a wife.
To sail along inside the ark,
The son picks a wife.

The wife picks the dog,
The wife picks the dog.
God sent them in to keep them safe,
The wife picks the dog.

The dog picks the cat,
The dog picks the cat.
God sent them in to keep them safe,
The dog picks the cat.

Add as many animals to this verse as you need to have all the children chosen.
Then sing this last verse.

We all leave the ark,
We all leave the ark.
God put a rainbow in the sky,
We all leave the ark.

Sarah
Genesis 15; 18:1-15; 21:1-21

A ninety-year-old woman having a baby? The thought is laughable! But Sarah was soon to discover that nothing is too hard for God. Although Sarah doubted God's promise of a son, her story offers us a clear example of God's promises coming true. In the face of what seemed impossible, God used Sarah to fulfill a powerful covenant.

Use the following activities to show children that we can trust God's promises and that God can use us to accomplish his mighty purposes.

Sarah's Smiles

Before this activity, spoon about one-fourth cup of white or pink frosting into a snack-sized resealable plastic bag. Squeeze the excess air from the bag and seal it. Snip a small piece from one corner of the bag to create a "pastry bag." You'll need one bag for every three children to share. Set out raisins and four-inch red string licorice.

Give each child a rice cake, then say: **The Bible tells us about a woman named Sarah who lived in a place that was hot and dry. Touch your rice cake and feel how dry the desert is.** Let children feel the rice cakes. **Sarah wanted to have a baby. But Sarah was very, very old. She was older than a grandma! So Sarah didn't think she would ever have a baby. That made her sad.**

One day, Sarah and her husband, Abraham, had some visitors. So they brought out lots of food and made a picnic for them. Let's add some tasty food to our snacks. Let children use the "pastry bags" to spread the frosting on their rice cakes. Collect the bags, then continue: **Sarah and Abraham had three visitors.** Let children place three raisins on their rice cakes, following the illustration in the margin.

They didn't know that the visitors were really messengers from God! As the visitors ate, they talked with Abraham. Sarah listened from inside their home. The visitors said, "In one year, your wife, Sarah, will have a baby boy." Sarah was surprised—that seemed silly! She was an old lady! In fact, Sarah was so surprised that she laughed at the very idea! Let children use the licorice to add a smile to the rice cake.

Even though Sarah thought it was silly, it was true! One year later, she *did* have a baby boy. She named him Isaac, which means "laughter." Let's eat these happy faces and remember Sarah, who laughed, and the baby she named "laughter."

Sing About Sarah

Teach children this song to the tune of "My Bonnie Lies Over the Ocean."

Old Sarah, she wanted a baby *(pretend to rock a baby)*,
But now she was ninety years old. *(Hold your back.)*
She shook her head sadly and figured *(shake head and frown)*,
"I won't have a baby to hold." *(Pretend to rock a baby.)*

Sarah, Sarah,
God promised to give you a son, a son! *(Pretend to rock a baby.)*
Sarah, Sarah,
God promised to give you a son! *(Pretend to rock a baby.)*

Abraham sat in the doorway
Of his tent that was near some big trees. *(Touch fingertips overhead to form "trees.")*
He looked and saw visitors coming. *(Hold hand above eyes.)*
He counted and saw, "One, two, three." *(Count on fingers.)*

(Whisper) But these men, these men *(cup hand to mouth as if sharing a secret)*,
Oh, they're really visitors from God, from God! *(Point up.)*
These men, God sent. *(Cup hand to mouth as if sharing a secret.)*
Oh, they're really visitors from God! *(Point up.)*

The visitors, they looked just like people
Who might need a drink and some food. *(Pretend to drink and eat.)*
So Abraham offered to feed them. *(Hold out hands.)*
He liked to be nice and not rude! *(Shake head.)*

"Sarah, Sarah *(cup hand to mouth as if calling)*,
Oh, bring out some food for our guests, our guests!" *(Motion "come on.")*
"Sarah, Sarah *(cup hand to mouth as if calling)*,
Oh, bring out some food for our guests!" *(Motion "come on.")*

The visitors sat and they chatted
With Abraham, when they were fed. *(Pretend to eat.)*
While inside old Sarah was listening. *(Cup hand to ear.)*
She couldn't believe what they said! *(Put hand over mouth in surprise.)*

"Your wife, Sarah,
Oh, she'll have a baby next year, next year!" *(Pretend to rock a baby.)*
"Your wife, Sarah,
Oh, she'll have a baby next year!" *(Pretend to rock a baby.)*

Well, Sarah she couldn't stop laughing! *(Hold belly and laugh.)*
But the words of the strangers were true! *(Nod head.)*
A year after they came to visit,
Baby Isaac was born—then she knew. *(Pretend to rock a baby.)*

Sarah, Sarah,
God promised to give you a son, a son! *(Pretend to rock a baby.)*
Sarah, Sarah,
God promised to give you a son! *(Pretend to rock a baby.)*

Baby Clay Play

Give each child a handful of modeling dough. Let children mold their dough into sculptures as you tell the following story.

The Bible tells us about a woman named Sarah who wanted a baby. God had told Sarah and her husband, Abraham, that their family would be very big. God said they would have as many family members as there are stars in the sky! Use your dough to make a star. Allow one minute for children to mold their dough. Then continue: But Abraham and Sarah didn't have any children. Not even one! Sarah got older and older. Pretty soon, she was older than a grandma! But still no baby. Shape your dough so it looks like a hand to show that Sarah's arms were empty, with no baby to hold. Allow one minute for children to mold their dough.

Continue: One day, three visitors came to visit Abraham and Sarah. They were really special messengers from God, but Abraham and Sarah thought they were just people like you and me. The men ate outside the tent, talking with Abraham. While they talked, Sarah listened from inside the tent. The visitors told Abraham, "When we come back next year, your wife Sarah will have a baby!" Sarah was so surprised that she laughed out loud! Shape your dough into a big happy face to remember that Sarah laughed.

Allow one minute for children to mold their dough. Then continue: But the messengers were right! In one year, Sarah had a special little boy named Isaac. The name Isaac means "he laughs." Sarah named him that because she was so happy and surprised to have a baby when she was so old. Use your dough to make a little baby to remember the little boy that Sarah had, just like God had promised. Let children shape their dough into baby-shapes, then allow them to take the dough home.

A Mother's Necklace

Set out eighteen-inch lengths of colorful yarn and a bowl of fruit ring cereal. You may want to put tape on the ends of the yarn so it will be easier for children to thread the cereal.

Say: The Bible tells us a story about a woman named Sarah. More than anything, Sarah wanted a baby. But Sarah didn't have any children—not even one. Take this empty string to show that Sarah's arms were empty. Give each child a piece of yarn.

God had told Sarah's husband that one day they would have a huge family. In fact, God said that their family would be so big, there would be as many family members as there are stars! Put a few pieces of yellow cereal on your string to remember God's promise about the stars. Let children add several pieces of yellow cereal, then continue: But the years went by and still no children. Sarah began to give up hope. After all, now she was ninety years old...that's much older than a grandma! And most grandmas don't have little babies! One day, three visitors came to see Sarah and her husband Abraham. Add three pieces of cereal to your string for the three visitors.

Let children add three pieces of cereal, then continue: These weren't just ordinary visitors...they were really special messengers sent from God. Sarah brought them some food and drink, then she went inside the tent. As the men talked with Abraham, she listened from inside. The men said, "In one year, we'll come back and your wife, Sarah, will have a baby." Sarah was so surprised, she laughed! That seemed impossible! But the men said, "Is anything too hard for the Lord?"

Well, those messengers were exactly right! **Add one piece of cereal for the one year Sarah waited.** Pause while children add the cereal. **In one year, she had a little baby boy! Add one piece of blue cereal for the baby boy.** Let children add a blue piece of cereal to their strings. **Sarah was so happy and surprised that she named her son Isaac, which means "he laughs." And when Isaac got married, he had lots of children. Add a few more pieces of cereal to your strings for all those children.** Pause. **And all of Isaac's children had children too. Add some more cereal for all those children.** Pause while children add more pieces of cereal.

Pretty soon, God's promise was true! **Sarah and Abraham had grandchildren and great-grandchildren and great-great-grandchildren—too many family members to count, just like the stars!** Hold up a full necklace. **Remember when Sarah didn't have any children at all? Now their family was big and full, just as God had promised.** Help children tie their necklaces around their necks. Be sure to allow enough slack for them to easily slip the necklaces on and off their necks.

Rebekah

Genesis 24

ebekah was the daughter of Abraham's nephew. Today, we would say she was Isaac's first cousin once removed. Abraham made his servant promise to go back to Abraham's hometown, to his relatives there, to find a wife for his son Isaac. Through God's guidance, the servant was drawn to Rebekah's willingness to care for him and his animals. He found out she was a relative of Abraham's and went to meet her parents. Rebekah's willingness to go with the servant overcame her parents' reluctance to send her so far away, and they agreed to allow her to marry Isaac.

Rebekah has become a hero among Bible women because she was a willing servant and became a mother to many. Help children see that being willing to serve others before you are asked is a job worthy of a hero.

A Journey to Nahor

This interactive story will get the children involved while learning the story of Rebekah. Each time you say the words "a wife for Isaac," have the children sing just these four words, "Here comes the bride."

Abraham was getting very old, and his son Isaac needed a good wife. Abraham told his faithful servant to go back to the town where he was born and find _a wife for Isaac_. Pause to have children sing, "Here comes the bride." **Abraham wanted his servant to find a nice girl from his hometown of Nahor and bring her back to marry Isaac.**

So Abraham's servant took ten camels and packed their backs with lots of supplies for the long journey. Choose ten children to pretend to be camels and come to the front of the class. Have the class help you count the camels as you send them crawling back to their seats. If you have a small class, have them count to ten on all their fingers.

Through the long hot desert, the servant, the camels, and all the servant's helpers walked. Have the kids stand up and sit down as they pretend to go up and down over the hills. **Over the sandy hills and down the other side, up and down, up and down they traveled to find _a wife for Isaac_.** Pause.

When they finally arrived in Nahor where Abraham had told his servant to find _a wife for Isaac_ (pause), **the servant made everyone stop and sit down by the well to wait. He asked God to send the right girl for Isaac.**

Soon it was time for all the women to come to the well for more water. How would the servant know who the right girl would be? As all the women came, the servant saw that there were big girls and little girls, tall women and short women. They were all beautiful! They would all make a nice _wife for Isaac_. Pause. **Should the servant just pick a bride by saying the rhyme, "One potato, two potato, three potato, four"?**

Oh, no! That would never be good enough. So the servant prayed and asked God to have the right girl for Isaac be the one who not only gave the servant water to drink, but would give all the camels lots and lots of water to drink without being asked.

Many beautiful and nice girls came to the well, but no one offered to give the poor thirsty camels any water. After all, it would take a long, long time to give all those thirsty camels water. That would be too much work!

Soon a young girl came to the well. She gave the servant water and then began to give all the camels water, too! Back and forth she went from the well to the camels with her pitcher of water until all the camels had plenty of water. Could this be the _wife for Isaac_? Pause. **The servant waited and was quiet as he watched her work so hard. She was so happy to serve them all. It was as if she didn't mind the hard work at all!**

The servant decided to find out who she was and ask her father if she could be the _wife for Isaac_. Pause.

Her name was Rebekah. When the servant met her family, they were very excited to hear all about Abraham and Isaac. Her father said she could go back with the servant to marry Isaac, so they loaded up the camels and away they went.

Through the hot desert, Rebekah, the servant, the camels, and all the servant's helpers walked. Have the kids stand up and sit down as they pretend to go up and down over the hills. **Over the sandy hills and down the other side, up and down, up and down they traveled with Rebekah, _the wife for Isaac_.** Pause.

One day Isaac was out in the field and saw them coming. He ran to meet them. Have kids slap their knees to make running sounds. When Isaac saw Rebekah, he knew this would be his wife. Isaac and Rebekah were married. Isaac and Rebekah were so happy! Abraham was happy and his servant was happy! They had a party and celebrated for a long time because God had found *a wife for Isaac*. Pause.

The Marriage Celebration

The children will enjoy singing this wedding song in celebration. Have the children link arms and dance in a circle crossing their legs over one another as they go around slowly. (This is similar to a Jewish dance.) Sing to the tune of "Rejoice in the Lord."

Abraham told his servant to go and get a wife.
Abraham told his servant to go and get a wife.
The servant obeyed and traveled far away.
The servant obeyed and traveled far away.

He asked God to show him a good and loving girl.
He asked God to show him a good and loving girl.
For Isaac, for Isaac, a wife he had to find.
For Isaac, for Isaac, a wife he had to find.

Many girls came to get water at the well.
Many girls came to get water at the well.
But only Rebekah did water the camels.
Bur only Rebekah did water the camels.

The servant asked her parents if he could take her back.
The servant asked her parents if he could take her back.
They traveled and traveled until they reached Isaac.
They traveled and traveled until they reached Isaac.

Isaac and Rebekah got married right away.
Isaac and Rebekah got married right away.
They danced and rejoiced and God was very pleased.
They danced and rejoiced and God was very pleased. Yeah!

Water the Camels Game

This game might best be played outdoors. At one end of the playing area, place an empty bucket, a bucket filled halfway with water, a cup, and netting for a pretend veil for Rebekah. You'll also need big cards with the numbers one through ten on them. Shuffle them and place them upside down on the opposite side of the playing area. Choose a child to be Abraham's servant who will stand near the buckets. Choose half of your children to stand by the number cards. They will be the women coming to the well. The rest of your class can be the camels and should be on their hands and knees near the servant.

Before beginning the game, say: **Long ago a man named Abraham wanted to find a good wife for his son Isaac. He sent his servant out to find the one God had chosen. The servant asked God that the woman who would give all ten of his camels water would be the right wife for Isaac.**

Then begin by having the "servant" call out to the "women," "Who will give *all* my camels water?" The first "woman" turns over one number card, runs to the buckets, and scoops that number of cups of water into the empty bucket while all the children help count the number of cups of water. Then the "woman" returns to the end of the line. The "servant" calls out again and the next "woman" turns over a card and waters that number of "camels." The game ends when the number ten is turned over. This child becomes Rebekah, waters all the "camels," and places the veil on her head. You can then have the children switch roles.

Remind children of how Rebekah willingly gave all the camels water with a happy smile.

Snack Time Training

Allow the children to experience serving each other like Rebekah willingly gave water to the servant and his camels. Have at least twenty animal crackers for each pair of children, small pitchers of juice for the kids to pour themselves, and small cups. Put only a small amount of juice in the pitcher so the children can feel successful without spilling any.

Begin by helping the children each find a partner. Then say: **Abraham was old and wanted to find a great wife for his son Isaac. So he sent his faithful servant back to the land where Abraham was born. The servant took ten camels with him.** Have children count out ten animal crackers and set the crackers in a pile. **The servant asked God to show him which woman would be a good wife for Isaac. His plan was that the woman who offered to get water for the** thirsty camels would be the right one. **Rebekah came and poured water for the servant and all the camels.** Have the children carefully pour a small amount of juice into cups and give it to their partner. **After talking to Rebekah's family, the servant took Rebekah back to be Isaac's wife. They had a big party to celebrate the wedding with lots of good things to eat and drink. Rebekah was kind to water the camels and brave to go back with the servant. You can be like Rebekah when you help others happily.** Allow the children to eat the crackers and drink the juice.

Jacob

Genesis 25–35

Jacob, the deceiver, became forgiven Israel, the father of the Hebrew nation. Through these stories and games, the children will learn about Jacob's big family and the wonders of forgiveness.

Round the Ground With Sounds

This is a noisy story. Let the children echo your sounds throughout the story.

Isaac and Rebekah were sad. *(Boohoo!)*

They wanted a baby. *(Goo, goo.)*

God gave them not one baby, but two sons. *(Yahoo!)*

Esau came out first and Jacob next. *(Wahhh!)*

Esau grew up as a mighty hunter. *(Make a bow motion and the sounds of arrows flying through the air.)*

But Jacob was a quiet man who liked to stay near the tents with his mother. *(Place your finger to lips—shh.)*

One day Jacob played a mean trick on Esau. *(Shake finger as if to say, "Naughty, naughty.")*

He stole something from his brother, Esau. *(Place hand over mouth and gasp.)*

Esau became very mad. *(Growl.)*

Jacob ran away from home. *(Run in place.)*

Jacob got married and had twelve boys. *(Count to twelve together.)*

Then it was time to go back home. Would Esau forgive Jacob for stealing from him after all those years? *(Chatter teeth together in fear.)*

Would Esau still be angry? *(Chatter teeth.)*

Jacob took his wives, children, and animals to meet his brother. *(Walk in place.)*

He had goats. *(Naa.)*

He had sheep. *(Baa.)*

He had camels. *(Snort, chew, chew.)*

He had cows. *(Moo.)*

And he had donkeys. *(Heehaw.)*

Then Jacob heard soldiers coming. *(Pound feet.)*

Oh, no! They were Esau's men. *(Pound feet louder.)*

Was Esau still mad? Was he coming to kill Jacob? *(Pound louder and faster.)*

No. Esau hugged his brother, Jacob. They kissed and cried happy tears. *(Kids hug each other.)*

Esau forgave Jacob.

Our mighty God forgives us and we can forgive others, too. *(Shake hands with each other.)*

Let's Forgive and Really Live

Play this action game to teach about forgiveness. Pair the class as "Esaus" and "Jacobs." The "Jacobs" will run to the other side of the room as the "Esaus" growl. Then the "Jacobs" will start walking slowly back toward their partners as all the children say the poem. After the poem, have the children switch roles and repeat the game.

Let's not fight. It isn't right. *(Shake finger.)*

Esau and Jacob, hug and make up. *(Hug each other.)*

Let's forgive. It's the way to live! *(Jump up.)*

A Pile of Rocks—A Story That Talks

Place three mounds of modeling clay on three chairs around the room, and give each child three small stones. Start by having all the children seated in a group, holding their stones.

Say: **There once was a man named Isaac.** Have children hold up one rock. **He had two sons, Esau and Jacob.** Have the children hold up the other two stones. **When the boys got older, Jacob was very mean to Esau.** Have the children gently click the two stones against each other. **Jacob ran away from home. He was sad, afraid, and all by himself. He put a rock under his head as a pillow. In his sleep,**

God talked to Jacob. God said, "I am your God. I am with you wherever you go." So Jacob set up a rock and said, "This is the house of God." Have the children get up and each put a rock in the first mound of modeling clay.

After a long time away, Jacob was going back home with his wives, children, and goats and sheep and camels. He set up another rock altar. This pile of rocks meant "the Lord will keep watch over us." Let the children put rocks on the next mound. And God did.

When Jacob heard that four hundred of his brother's men were coming, he was scared! He cried to God, "Save me!" God did. Jacob set up another altar of rocks. This time it meant "God is mighty." Have children put rocks on the last mound. God saved Jacob and his family. God changed Jacob's name to Israel. Jacob, now called Israel, knew that God is real. You can be sure that God is real for you also. Here is a rock of your own to remind you that you can ask for forgiveness and that God will help you.

Gifts Galore

While the children create this tasty treat, they will have fun learning the story of Jacob's reunion with his brother, Esau. For each child, you will need a paper plate and a plastic knife. On the plate place a stalk of celery, a dollop of creamy peanut butter, several jelly beans, and two graham bears. If you think nut allergies may be a problem, substitute flavored cream cheese for the peanut butter.

Say: Long ago, twin boys were born. But one of the boys, Jacob, played a very bad trick on his brother, Esau. Esau was very angry and Jacob ran away because he was afraid of Esau. Put your bears far apart on your plate.

Jacob got married and had many children. After many years away, he wanted to go back to his home. But he was still not sure if Esau was still mad at him.

It was a long road back to his home. The celery stick will be like the road that Jacob and all his family and all his sheep and cows and camels had to travel. The peanut butter will be the dirt that covered the road. Allow the children time to spread the peanut butter on the celery stalk. The peanut butter will be a little easier to spread if the celery has been patted dry. This will be messy so it might be helpful to have wet paper towels to wipe hands. Jacob was so worried that Esau would still be mad at him that he sent his servants out in front of him with gifts for Esau. Put one jelly bean on the road to be the servants of Jacob. Add another jelly bean for the goats Jacob sent as a gift to Esau. And now add another jelly bean for the sheep Jacob sent as a gift. We need to add another jelly bean for the cows, and still another one for all the donkeys he sent. That is a lot of gifts.

Jacob was very sorry for what he had done to his brother. God had blessed Jacob, and now Esau forgave Jacob. Esau gave Jacob a big hug. Let your little bears give each other a hug, and then let's eat our snack and remember that God wants us to be ready to say we are sorry when we do wrong.

Fingers and Feet

You can count on this finger play for fun. Put up a finger for each son of Jacob.

Jacob was the father of twelve strong boys.
Reuben and Simeon were his joys. (Hold up two fingers.)
Levi, Judah, then came Gad. (Hold up rest of fingers and thumb.)
Five little boys and Jacob was glad! (Wiggle five fingers.)
Naphtali was born and then came Dan. (On other hand, hold up two fingers.)
Issachar and Zebulun joined the clan. (Hold up two more fingers.)
Asher was next. They grew to men. (Hold out thumb and raise hands high.)
But Jacob had twelve sons, not just ten.
Ten fingers are used, but we're not through. (Wiggle ten fingers.)
For two more sons, what will we do? (Palms up, shrug shoulders.)
I have an idea I think is neat.
For eleven and twelve, we'll use our feet!
Jacob became the father of Joseph and Ben. (Lift up one foot and then the other.)
Let's count back to do it over again.
Twelve, eleven (fold legs up), ten, nine, eight, seven, six. (Put fingers down on one hand as you count.)
Isn't this a funny trick?
Five, four, three, two, one, and zero. (Put fingers down on other hand as you count.)
Jacob was a Bible hero!

Joseph
Genesis 37:12-36; 41–45

The story of Joseph can encourage little ones to forgive each other and to trust God to turn bad into good. Use these activities to remind children that they can forgive, just as Joseph did!

Puppet Play

Children will have fun using puppets to act out the story of Joseph and his brothers. Before the story, create a simple Joseph puppet for each child in class. For each puppet, stuff a paper wad inside a small paper lunch bag, and use yarn to tie off the bag beneath the paper wad to make the head. Set out colorful markers, tape, and plain paper or cloth squares. Make a puppet for yourself also. Lead kids in the following actions.

Say: **Jacob lived in the land of Canaan. He had many sons, but Joseph was his favorite.** Have each child draw a face on his or her puppet. **Jacob loved Joseph so much that he gave him a beautiful coat of many colors to wear. Joseph's brothers were very jealous.** Let each child use markers to decorate a sheet of paper or a cloth square as Joseph's coat. Help children wrap the coats around the puppet. Secure the coats with small pieces of tape.

One day, Joseph went to visit his brothers who were watching over their sheep. Have puppet pretend to walk. **Joseph's brothers took his coat, and threw him down into an empty well.** Remove the puppet's coat, and place the puppet on the floor. **Then they sold him as a slave to people who were traveling to Egypt.** Wave goodbye. **They put animal blood on Joseph's coat.** Crumple up the coat. **Then they went home and told their father that a wild animal had killed Joseph. Jacob was very sad.** Rub your eyes as if crying.

God took care of Joseph in Egypt and made him very powerful. In fact, he was in charge of all of the food in the land. Hold the puppet up high. God told Joseph about Pharaoh's dream: Soon there wouldn't be enough food to feed all the people. So Joseph put lots and lots of food away to save. Sure enough, soon there was no more food to eat. Rub your tummy. Joseph's brothers were very hungry, and they came to Egypt to ask for food for their family. They were afraid when they saw that it was Joseph who was in charge of the food. Cover your eyes. But Joseph forgave his brothers and gave them all the food they wanted. And the family lived together again! Wave the puppet in the air.

Coat of Many Colors

Before this activity, set out several colors of icing in snack-sized resealable plastic bags. Remove the air from the bags and seal them. Snip a small piece from one corner to create a "pastry bag." You will also need a Life Savers-type piece of candy for each child. Give each child a large gingerbread man on a paper plate. The children will be making colorful coats for their figures, just as Jacob gave a beautiful coat of many colors to his favorite son, Joseph. Children will use plastic knives to work on the coats (Small pastry brushes work well also.)

Say: Jacob had twelve sons, but he loved Joseph more than the others. To show his love, Jacob gave Joseph a beautiful, colorful coat. We don't know exactly what it looked like, but the Bible tells us it had many colors. It may have had stripes or dots, so you may put the colors on the coat of your Joseph cookie anyway you would like. Allow time for children to decorate the coat area on the cookie. Joseph's brothers did not like him at all and finally they decided to get rid of him. They took his coat away from him and sold him as a slave. After he was gone, they messed up his coat so it looked like a wild animal had attacked Joseph. Have the children take the knives or brushes and "mess up" the frosting on the cookies.

Even though it seemed to be a very bad thing to be sold as a slave, God had a wonderful plan for Joseph. He became a great leader in Egypt where he had once been a slave. Have the children put a small amount of frosting at the top of the head of the cookie. Add a small round candy for a crown. He was able to save a lot of food for a time when many people were very hungry. Even his own brothers came to him to buy food, and Joseph gave them food to eat, just as you will eat your cookies.

When children finish decorating their cookies, lead them in a prayer thanking God for taking care of Joseph and his brothers. Then let children enjoy their snacks!

Coat Capers

Children will delight in this fast-paced game! Bring in a colorful coat in a size that will fit your children. (If you have a large class, bring in two coats and have kids play the game in two groups.) Place the coat on a chair at one end of the room. Have children line up on the other side of the room. Teach children this rhyme:

Joseph in your coat so bright,
Please forgive and do what's right.

To begin, say the first line of the story. The first child in the line will repeat the above rhyme, and then run to the chair, put on the coat, and run back to the line. When you say the next line of the story, the second child will say the rhyme to the child wearing the coat. The first child will remove the coat and hand it to the second child. The second child will put on the coat, run across the room and around the chair, then run back to the line. The next child will repeat the rhyme, after the next line of the story, and the process will continue.

Story lines:

Joseph's brothers were so mean.
Joseph had to be a slave.
God had a big plan for Joseph.
Joseph saved a lot of food in the new country.
Joseph's brothers needed food and came to Joseph.

If you have a large class, repeat the story lines until each child has had a turn to wear the coat. When each child has had a turn, lead children in this final rhyme:

Joseph in his coat so bright;
He forgave and did what's right!

Forgiveness Song

Teach children this song to the tune of "Mary Had a Little Lamb."

Joseph had a coat so glad, coat so glad, coat so glad.
Joseph had a coat so glad.
It made his brothers mad.

They sold him to those passing by, passing by, passing by.
They sold him to those passing by
And told their dad a lie.

In Egypt, Joseph did so good, did so good, did so good.
In Egypt, Joseph did so good.
He took care of the food.

His brothers came to ask for food, ask for food, ask for food.
His brothers came to ask for food.
They were in a hungry mood.

Joseph could have sent them away, sent them away, sent them away.
Joseph could have sent them away,
But instead he said, "Please stay."

He forgave them for how bad they'd been, bad they'd been, bad they'd
    been.
He forgave them for how bad they'd been,
And they were a family again!

Miriam

Exodus 2:1-10

Miriam was Moses' big sister. We find her for the first time in the Bible watching over her little brother and experiencing God's care and mercy for him and their family. She is known for her trust in God and joyful praise she gave to God when he freed them from Egypt.

Where Is Miriam?

Preschoolers will enjoy singing this song to the tune of "Frére Jacques" and doing this fun finger play.

Where is Miriam? Where is Miriam? *(Hand over eyes looking around.)*
There she is! There she is! *(Point to friends.)*
See the little baby. *(Place fingers in front of eyes and peek through.)*
That's her brother Moses. *(Make circles touching fingers to thumbs and place in front of eyes.)*
Be brave, Miriam! Be brave, Miriam!

Where is Miriam? Where is Miriam? *(Hand over eyes looking around.)*
There she is! There she is! *(Point to friends.)*
See the little basket. *(Hold arms out in large circle.)*
Moses sleeps inside it. *(Make a circle by holding first finger and thumb together on one hand, then use first finger on other hand to point into the circle.)*
Be brave, Miriam! Be brave, Miriam!

Where is Miriam? Where is Miriam? *(Hand over eyes looking around.)*
There she is! There she is! *(Point to friends.)*

The basket's in the river. *(Use one arm to make wave motions from one side to the other.)*

Where will Moses go? *(Shrug shoulders as if not knowing.)*

Be brave, Miriam! Be brave, Miriam!

Where is Miriam? Where is Miriam? *(Hand over eyes looking around.)*

There she is! There she is! *(Point to friends.)*

Hiding in the bushes. *(Crouch down and hold hands over face.)*

Looking after Moses. *(Stand up and lean over as if looking down on something.)*

Be brave, Miriam! Be brave, Miriam!

Where is Miriam? Where is Miriam? *(Hand over eyes looking around.)*

There she is! There she is! *(Point to friends.)*

The princess lifts up Moses. *(Hold hands up in air as if holding something up.)*

Will she want to keep him? *(Shrug shoulders as if not knowing.)*

Be brave, Miriam! Be brave, Miriam!

Where is Miriam? Where is Miriam? *(Hand over eyes looking around.)*

There she is! There she is! *(Point to friends.)*

Talking to the princess. *(Kneel and fold hands as if begging.)*

Their mom will be the helper. *(Hug self.)*

Be brave, Miriam! Be brave, Miriam! *(Make praying hands.)*

Following Moses

Have the children stand in a line with at least one body width between them.

Begin by saying: **A long time ago, God used a girl named Miriam as part of a big plan. Miriam's mother had a baby boy and needed to keep him safe. She made a basket for him and put him in the river. Miriam had a big job to do. God helped make her brave. She followed the basket with Moses in it wherever it went. The first person here in line will be Moses and the line of people will be the weeds at the edge of the river. Moses will crawl in and out of the weeds. The second person here will be Miriam. Miriam must follow Moses wherever he goes.** When the pair reach the other end of the line (the princess's house) they both jump up and shout, "God made Miriam brave, and kept Moses safe." They both join the end of the line and the next two people at the front of the line become Moses and Miriam.

Miriam in the Bulrushes Snack

To make Miriam in the bulrushes, you'll need shredded wheat crackers, soft cream cheese, black pitted olives, plastic knives, and string cheese. Give each child one shredded wheat cracker. Begin by saying: **Moses was born during a very hard time. Moses' family and all of their people were slaves. The king did not want there to be any more boy slaves so he tried to kill all the baby boys.**

But God had a great plan. Moses' mother got a basket. These crackers look a little bit like a basket. His mother put tar on the basket to keep the water out. We are going to put this cream cheese on ours. Allow children to spread the cream cheese on their crackers. **Then Moses' mother put him in the basket. We're going to use these olives to be like the baby Moses.** Give each child an olive to place on top of the cream cheese.

The mother put the basket with baby Moses in it into the river. Then Moses' big sister had a very important and hard job. She watched the basket to see that Moses was safe. The basket was in tall weeds at the edge of the river. We are going to tear pieces off our cheese to be like the weeds that hid the basket. Have the children tear off strings of the cheese and lay over the cracker and olive.

Miriam was brave and followed the basket along the river. Have the children move their cracker with one hand and use two fingers of other hand to "walk after" the cracker. **The daughter of the king found the basket and picked up the baby.** Have children pick up the crackers. **Now Miriam did the bravest thing ever! She walked up to the princess and ask her if she needed help taking care of the baby. And that was all part of God's big plan.**

You can each be a part of God's big plans too. Now let's eat our snack and remember that God uses kids in his big plans.

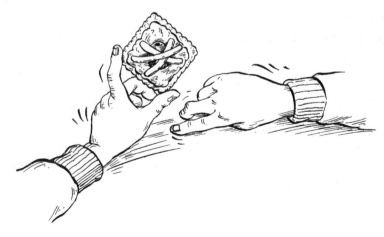

A Prayer for Help

Teach the children this prayer and have them follow the motions. Have them say it with you several times. Then form two groups and have the groups alternate saying the lines.

Dear God,

I know that Moses' mom was worried and hid baby Moses in the river. *(Wring your hands.)*

You helped her to know what to do. *(Point up.)*

Baby Moses was crying. *(Rub your eyes.)*

You helped him to be safe. *(Point up.)*

Big sister Miriam was scared. *(Cover your eyes.)*

You helped her to be brave. *(Point up.)*

You will help us, too. *(Hug self.)*

You are my helper; please help me not be afraid. *(Point up.)*

Thank you, God. Amen. *(Hug self.)*

Moses
Exodus 3–14

There are few greater heroes than Moses when it comes to obeying God. Not only did Moses follow God's command to lead his people out of slavery, but he also set a wonderful example of faithfulness for all of us to follow. Preschoolers can learn the joy that comes in obedience and the rewards of faithfulness as they learn about the man who led the Hebrews out of bondage and received the rules that God wants us to live by.

Moses Leads God's People

Children will enjoy acting out this action rhyme that shows the great things that Moses did. Practice by asking preschoolers to repeat the words and actions of the story.

Moses was a baby floating out to sea *(cradle arms)*,
Caught by Pharaoh's daughter, which was great, you must agree! *(Bend over and pretend to pick up baby and hold him in the air.)*
When he found out he was a Hebrew and a part of God's great plan *(point to God above)*,
Moses climbed up on the mountain to listen as a man. *(Climb in place, then put a hand to your ear.)*
God instructed Moses on this very special day *(hold one finger up in the air)*,
"Go and free my people, and I will show you the way." *(Point far away.)*
Moses did whatever God asked, and obeyed all his commands *(bow head)*
By going back to Pharaoh with all of God's demands. *(Put hands on hips.)*
"Let God's people go!" Moses said with all his might. *(Make strong arms.)*

He showed that God was serious with plagues throughout the fight.
(Make a serious face and hold up ten fingers.)

Pharaoh let the people go, afraid of what else God would do! *(Make a scared face and shoo away from your body with your hands.)*

So Moses led his people away to a land that was promised and true.
(Spread arms out.)

The people marched across the desert, with Pharaoh close behind.
(March in place.)

But with God's help, the sea did part to help the people find *(extend arms together and clasp hands, then separate them up to the sides and in the air)*

A land that was safe, away from harm, showing that God was kind.
(Hug yourself.)

Back up the mountain Moses went, as God told him to do *(climb in place)*

To get God's Ten Commandments to follow through and through.
(Hold up ten fingers.)

Split Sea Snack

Preschoolers can learn about the great things God did through Moses as they eat a snack! Make a batch of blueberry gelatin squares by following the directions on the box. Cut them into enough squares so that each child can have one. You will also need two small paper muffin cups and teddy bear crackers for each child.

As you tell the story, children can use the snack items to act out what you say.

Moses obeyed God by leading his people out of slavery and into a new land. Select one teddy bear cracker to represent Moses. Put the rest of "God's people" into a muffin cup.

But Pharaoh was angry about losing his slaves, so he started after them as they crossed the desert! Select another cracker to represent Pharaoh and put his "army" into another muffin cup.

Moses led the people away from Pharaoh and across the desert. But then they came to a gigantic sea and didn't know what to do! Slide the muffin cup with Moses and his people up to the blue gelatin square.

Moses trusted God and knew he would help, so he raised his staff into the air and told the sea to part! Break your gelatin square in half.

Moses and God's people quickly crossed through the split sea. Move Moses and his people between each half of the gelatin.

When God's people were safely across, Moses lowered his hands and the sea went back together, covering Pharaoh's army! The muffin cup with Moses and his people are on one side of the gelatin, while Pharaoh and his people are in between the halves. Bring the two halves together and place over the muffin cup with Pharaoh's army. Enjoy your snack!

God! I'll Obey You!

Teach this song to the tune of "Jesus Loves Me" so kids will learn about how Moses obeyed God.

God loved Moses, Moses knew that *(Cross arms over chest.)*
After they had a great big chat. *(Put hands on each side of mouth.)*
He led the people from slavery *(wipe brow with hand)*
Showing God his bravery. *(Show strong arms.)*
God! I'll obey you! *(Point to God and salute.)*
God! I'll obey you! *(Repeat.)*
God! I'll obey you! *(Repeat.)*
Just like Moses did! *(Cross arms over chest.)*

Moses Surprise Box

Kids will enjoy the story of Moses as they discover a box filled with surprises about him! You will need a box with the following inside: a small baby doll, a crown, plastic construction blocks, a rubber snake, a container with small gravel, a clear container of water and red food coloring, a blue bowl and several small army men, and a tablet of clay. Feel free to be creative and add other items you have available!

Moses was a little baby, who was rescued by the king's daughter, who found him floating in a basket in the river. Reach into the box and take out the small baby doll. Have a child come to the front and hold the doll. The king's daughter raised Moses as if he was her own son. Reach into the box and take out the crown. Choose a child to come up and wear the crown. The king had many slaves to build him a beautiful city. Take out the blocks from the box. Have several children build something from them. The king was mean to the slaves and made them work hard! But they were God's people and God promised to send them someone who would help! God told Moses to help the slaves escape from Egypt. God promised to help Moses.

So Moses went back to the king and told the king to let God's people go! He tried to scare the king by turning his walking stick into a snake! Take out the rubber snake and let one child hold it up in front of all the others. But the king was not afraid. So God helped Moses show the king God's power! God sent down rain and hail! Take out the container of gravel. Let the kids take a handful of gravel and listen as it's dropped into the bottom of the container. God changed the water into blood! Take out the container of water and the food coloring. Pour several drops of red food coloring into your clear container and stir. Finally, after many other bad things happened, the king let the slaves go. The people were very happy!

But as God's people traveled away from Egypt, the king changed his mind and sent his army after them! Take out the army men and let several children hold them while they march in place. The people were afraid, especially when they came to the sea and could not get across it! Take out the blue bowl and have a child come and turn it upside down. But God helped Moses again. God opened the water so God's people could cross! Have a child flip bowl right side up. But then the army crossed too! Have the children with the army men put them into the bowl. Before the army men got to the other side, the water came back and covered up the mean army men. Turn the bowl back upside down with army men underneath it. Moses led God's people to a mountain where God gave him ten special rules. Take out the clay tablet. Have a child hold it up. These are the rules God wants everyone to obey. Moses had a lot of very hard things to do, but God was there with him, and Moses listened to God. Let children put the items back in the box one at a time and tell what each item meant.

Rahab
Joshua 2:1-21; 6:25

The story of Rahab shows a woman acknowledging God as the one true God. Rahab's brave actions saved the lives of Joshua's spies and saved her entire extended family from harm. Little ones can learn from Rahab's example to also see the power of God and the rewards of brave choices. These activities will help your children learn about brave Rahab—an interesting addition to the story of the walls of Jericho.

Rahab Hides Two Men

Children will enjoy the motions with this story. Read the story and do the motions. The children will easily follow your lead.

Joshua sent out two spies. *(Stand up and point with arms and first finger straight out.)*

They went to Jericho. *(Walk in place.)*

They went to Rahab's house. *(Pretend to knock on a door.)*

Rahab said, "Come in!" *(Motion to "come in" with arm and hand.)*

She took them to the roof. *(Climb up stairs in place.)*

She hid them under straw. *(Pretend to place straw over men.)*

Soldiers came to find the men. *(Frown and pretend to hold a spear while looking around with other hand to eyes.)*

But they couldn't find them there. *(Shrug your shoulders.)*

So the soldiers looked outside Jericho. *(Walk in place.)*

The spies said, "You saved our lives!" *(Hold hands high in the air.)*

Rahab said, "Please save my family *(fold hands together as if pleading)*

When Jericho falls." *(Hold hands in the air, and then wiggle hands down to the ground.)*

The spies said, "We will!" *(Nod head up and down.)*

Just put this red rope in your window." *(Pretend to put cord out a window.)*

So when God's people came to Jericho, Rahab and her family were safe. *(Wrap your arms around yourself.)*

A Brave Song

Children will enjoy learning this song about Rahab's brave acts. Sing the words to the tune of "This Old Man."

Two spies came *(hold up two fingers)*
To Jericho. *(Make an outline of a big wall with arms.)*
Soldiers looked both high and low. *(Hold hand over eyes and look around.)*
With a pile of straw *(pretend to lay down a pile of something)*
And a cord of scarlet red *(pull hands apart as if holding a cord between them)*,
Rahab showed how brave she was. *(Place hands over heart.)*

Two spies hid *(hold up two fingers)*
In the straw. *(Hold arms over head and crouch down.)*
Soldiers looked and never saw. *(Walk in place and hold hands over eyes looking around.)*
With a pile of straw *(pretend to lay down a pile of something)*
And a cord of scarlet red *(pull hands apart as if holding a cord between them)*,
Rahab showed how brave she was. *(Place hands over heart.)*

Two spies left. *(Hold up two fingers.)*
They climbed down *(climb hand over hand as if down a rope)*,
Out the window, out of town. *(Run in place.)*
With a pile of straw *(pretend to lay down a pile of something)*
And a cord of scarlet red *(pull hands apart as if holding a cord between them)*,
Rahab showed how brave she was. *(Place hands over heart.)*

God's people came *(march in place)*
To the wall. *(Make a big outline of a wall with arms.)*
The family stayed safe in the fall. *(Wrap arms around self.)*
With a pile of straw *(pretend to lay down a pile of something)*
And a cord of scarlet red *(pull hands apart as if holding a cord between them)*,
Rahab showed how brave she was. *(Place hands over heart.)*

Out the Window Snacks

While building an edible window, children will hear the story of Rahab and the spies. Set out plates with mini marshmallows and stick pretzels for small groups of children (three to five children per group). Also have enough pieces of red string licorice for each child to have one. Have children follow your example.

Pick up one marshmallow. **Joshua sent out two spies.** Pick up two pretzel sticks and stick them into the marshmallow to form a right angle. **They met Rahab.** Add a marshmallow to the horizontal pretzel. **Soldiers looked for the spies.** Add a marshmallow to the vertical pretzel. **Rahab took the spies to the roof.** Add a pretzel going "up" from the horizontal pretzel. **She covered them with straw.** Add a pretzel across the top. **The soldiers looked for the spies somewhere else.** Add the final marshmallow to the corner to connect the last two pretzels. **Rahab helped the spies escape out the window of her house.** Hold up the completed square and look through it to show it is a window. **Then she hung a red rope in her window so that Joshua and all his men could keep her safe when the walls of Jericho fell down.** Give each child a string of the red licorice to hang through the window. Allow children to eat.

Shapes of Jericho

Have the following large shapes cut out of paper and placed around the room: square, rectangle, circle, and triangle. Then say: **I am going to tell you a story and each time you hear the name of a shape in this story, I want you to go to where you see that shape in our room. This will let you practice listening and obeying, just like we need to listen to and obey God. Let's begin.**

Joshua and his men sat in a *circle*. They decided that two men should go to check out the city of Jericho. These two spies went to the big *rectangle* walls of Jericho. The walls were very tall and there were towers that had *triangle* tops. They found a lady who said she would help them. Her name was Rahab. She let them come into her house through the *rectangle-shaped* door. Soldiers came looking for the spies. They walked in a *circle* all though Rahab's house but couldn't find the spies. Rahab had taken them up to the *square* roof of her house, and hidden them under a big *circle* of straw. After the soldiers left to look for the spies somewhere else, Rahab let the spies crawl down a rope from her *square* window to get away. The spies promised to keep Rahab and all her family safe because she was so brave and helped them.

All Together Now

The children will love to shout out the responsive line after each section of the story of Rahab. Practice the line, "Be brave, Rahab. God will keep you safe" with the children several times so they will be able to shout it out at the end of each section.

God's people were moving to a special land. They sent out spies to the city of Jericho in that land.

(Children shout.) **Be brave, Rahab! God will keep you safe!**

The spies needed a place to stay inside the city. They asked Rahab to help them.

(Children shout.) **Be brave, Rahab! God will keep you safe!**

The king of Jericho found out that spies were in the city. He sent soldiers to Rahab's house to find the spies.

(Children shout.) **Be brave, Rahab! God will keep you safe!**

Rahab hid the spies up on the roof of her house under a pile of straw.

(Children shout.) **Be brave, Rahab! God will keep you safe!**

Rahab knew God's people would all come to Jericho. She knew that the Lord was the true God. She wanted to keep her family safe when God's people came.

(Children shout.) **Be brave, Rahab! God will keep you safe!**

Rahab asked the spies to help keep her family safe, since she had helped to keep them safe. They said "Just hang a red rope out of your window, and we will know which house is yours."

(Children shout.) **Be brave, Rahab! God will keep you safe!**

When it was safe, Rahab let the two spies climb down a rope from her window, and out of the city. They went back to report all they had learned.

(Children shout.) **Be brave, Rahab! God will keep you safe!**

When God's people did come to Jericho, they saw the red rope in the window of Rahab's house and everyone in her house was safe.

(Children shout.) **Be brave, Rahab! God will keep you safe!**

Joshua

Exodus 24:13-18; Numbers 13–14:9;
Joshua 3–4:9; 24:14-18

Joshua was known for his deep trust in the Lord. He was chosen by God to complete Moses' work, leading Israel into the Promised Land. The following activities will help your children learn what a trusting servant Joshua was and how he helped the people of Israel.

Moses' Friend and Servant

Have children form a circle. Introduce Joshua to the children by learning this song to the tune of "Bingo."

Moses had a special friend and Joshua was his name-o.
Joshua was Moses' friend.
He served and helped him too.
Joshua was Moses' friend.
God chose him to help Moses.

After learning the words to the song, choose a child to be Moses. Have "Moses" stand in the middle of the circle. Have the children walk around in a circle while singing the song. During the song, have "Moses" choose another child to be Joshua. Have the children sing the song again with both children in the middle. At the end of the song, have "Joshua" and "Moses" bow, then choose another child to play the part of Moses.

Joshua and Caleb Are Spies

Use fruit to make an edible Joshua character. Give each child a small apple, nine grapes, and five toothpicks. Note: If you have younger children in your group, you may want to cut the grapes in half to prevent a choking hazard. As you tell the story below, have each child put his or her "Joshua" together, following your directions. After the story, take apart the character and let the children eat the snack. (Retrieve the toothpicks before anyone is allowed to eat.)

God told Moses to send some men to explore a new land. Moses thought and thought. He used his head to choose twelve men to explore the land. You choose one grape to put on a toothpick. Put the grape on one end of the toothpick to be Joshua's head and poke the other end of the toothpick into the top of the apple. Pause while the children follow your instructions.

The twelve men walked and walked to find the new land. Put two grapes on a toothpick and put it into the bottom of the apple for a leg and foot. Pause for the children to do this. **The men walked and explored for forty days, and then walked back home. The men chose some grapes to take back to Moses. Put two grapes on another toothpick and put it into the bottom of the apple for the other leg.** Allow a moment for children to follow your instructions. **Caleb and Joshua pointed to the land and told Moses, "God wants us to have this land. He will be with us. We should go up and take this land." Choose two grapes. Put them on a toothpick for an arm and hand. Poke the toothpick into the apple on one side.** Pause for the children to do this. **But the others said, "The fruit of the land is good, but the people are too big and strong for us. We cannot take their land." Use two more grapes; put them on a toothpick for an arm and hand. Poke the toothpick into the other side of the apple.** Pause for the children to do this. **Joshua and Caleb trusted God. They knew that he would help them take the land that God wanted them to have.**

To the Promised Land

Joshua had the pleasure of leading the Israelites into the Promised Land because of his faithfulness. Sing the following song to the tune of "London Bridge." Choose two children to form an arch by linking hands and holding them above their heads. Have all the other children walk under the arch, in a circle, as you sing the song. The children forming the arch should drop their arms on the last line of each verse, to "catch" one of the children. Then that child will trade places with one of the children who formed the arch.

Joshua went to the Promised Land,
Promised Land,
Promised Land.
Joshua went to the Promised Land.
He led God's people.

Joshua walked through the Jordan River,
Jordan River,
Jordan River.
Joshua walked through the Jordan River.
He led God's people.

Joshua fought the battles, too.
Battles here,
Battles there.
Joshua fought the battles, too.
He led God's people.

Joshua gave out all the land,
All the land,
All the land.
Joshua gave out all the land.
Gave it to God's people.

Going on a Field Trip

Take the children on a "field trip" to the Promised Land. Use this variation of "Going on a Bear Hunt." Have the children make walking sounds by alternately patting each knee with each hand. As they "walk," tell them the story of Joshua. Have them repeat each line after you say it. At the end of each verse have them shout, "Be brave, Joshua!"

Goin' to the Promised Land.
I see a river.
Can't go over.
Can't go under it.
Have to go through it.
(Children shout.) "Be brave, Joshua!"

Goin' to the Promised Land.
I see a city.
It has a high wall.
Can't go over it.
Can't go under it.
Have to go around it.
(Children shout.) "Be brave, Joshua!"

Goin' to the Promised Land.
I see another city.
Can't go over it.
Can't go under it.
Can't walk around it.
Have to fight for it.
(Children shout.) "Be brave, Joshua!"

Goin' to the Promised Land.
God gave us all the land.
We can live here.
We can build here.
We will stay here.
(Children shout.) "Be brave, Joshua!"

Deborah
Judges 4–5

eborah is especially important for children to know because she was the only woman mentioned in Scripture that God appointed as judge over the children of Israel. She is especially remembered because she listened and trusted God's words that Israel would win the battle and defeat the king of Canaan who held Israel again in slavery. On the day of battle, Deborah, a woman, led the children of Israel into victory.

A Wise Woman

This is a fun rhyme for the children to do as a finger play. Give it an extra twist by combining it with shadow puppetry. Use five small gingerbread people cookies (or teddy bear crackers) placed on an overhead during the appropriate places as the children say the rhyme.

Long, long ago, God's people were sad. *(Hold up all fingers, then curve them down as if sad.)*

They were ruled by a man who was very bad. *(Hold up one finger.)*

But over near Ramah was one who was wise. *(Point away.)*

Deborah listened to God and never told lies. *(Point up, then put finger on lips.)*

People would come to her with problems they had. *(Fold arms across chest and pout.)*

Deborah would help them, then they would be glad. *(Arms in the air and smile.)*

She called for a soldier to fight the bad king. *(Motion with arm for someone to come.)*

God gave them victory, then to God they did sing! *(Arms in the air and shout, "Hooray!")*

So if you listen to God, you can be wise. *(Cup hand around ear.)*

Do what God says and never tell lies. *(Nod head.)*

Deborah's Dance to God

The children will enjoy singing and dancing to God as Deborah and Barak did after they won the battle. Each child will need a piece of brightly colored crepe paper ribbon about two to three feet long. Another option is to have children make this craft to take home by taping a fabric ribbon to the end of a one-foot dowel.

As they sing have the children skip in a circle waving their ribbons from side to side. When they get to the line "all around the city," have them stop and spin in a circle holding the ribbon above their head. Sing this song to the tune of "Skip to My Lou."

Deborah heard God and obeyed him too.
Deborah heard God and obeyed him too.
Deborah heard God and obeyed him too.
All around the city.

Deborah and Barak led the men.
Deborah and Barak led the men.
Deborah and Barak led the men.
All around the city.

Dance to the Lord and sing his praise.
Dance to the Lord and sing his praise.
Dance to the Lord and sing his praise
All around the city.

A Deborah Snack Creation

To create a Deborah snack, each child will need a wooden skewer, one-half of a hot dog, a lettuce leaf, rectangular slice of cheddar cheese, and a cherry tomato. First have the children push their hot dog down onto the skewer allowing about two to three inches of space at the top for her "head." Say: **Once there was a lady named Deborah. She listened to God.** Place the point of the skewer through the center of the lettuce leaf and push it down to drape over her hot-dog body. **So God gave her** great wisdom to help people with their problems. Have rectangular slices of cheese cut to use as arms by placing the skewer in the center of the rectangle and pushing it down on top of the lettuce. **Deborah asked a brave soldier named Barak to fight a bad king to help the people. When the bad king was gone, Deborah and Barak sang praises to God.** The finishing touch is the tomato for her head placed at the end.

Let the kids walk their "Deborahs" around the table as you remind them of how God made Deborah wise and brave and she won the battle that day. Thank God for Deborah and the snack God provided for them and let them enjoy.

Deborah the Hero

Have fun singing this song to the tune of "Rejoice in the Lord." Sing the song through once, then add the motions.

Deborah was a mighty judge
Who listened to God all day. *(Stretch up toward God with hand behind ear.)*
The people brought their problems
In many, many ways. *(Put both hands on head and shake head.)*
She listened and answered *(stretch to one side with hand behind ear)*
And told them what to do. *(Point both index fingers at mouth, then point away from mouth as you stretch to the other way.)*
She listened and answered *(Stretch to one side with hand behind ear.)*
And told them what to do. *(Point both index fingers at mouth then point away from mouth as you stretch to the other way.)*

Then one day God told her *(point up to God)*
The king would end his rule. *(Point arms down and move outward, similar to the baseball signal for "safe.")*
Barak made her come with him. *(Motion for someone to come.)*
But he was such a fool. *(Point to head and shake it "no.")*
A hero, a hero *(show one strong arm then the other),*
God made her on that day! *(Point up to God.)*
A hero, a hero *(show one strong arm then the other),*
God made her on that day! *(Point up to God.)*

Gideon
Judges 6:11–7:25

God made Gideon a hero in the sight of the children of Israel and gave him victory over the Midianites in the promised land of Canaan. The process and patience God used to build Gideon's trust are seen through the many ways Gideon asked God to prove himself. Each time God showed Gideon what he could do and each time Gideon believed just a little bit more, until it was battle time. Gideon went into battle with only three hundred men and no weapons. Because of God's promise, the enemy ran away and Gideon and his three hundred men took over the city. Gideon became a hero to the children of Israel from that day on.

Mighty, Mighty Gideon

Here's a fun rhyming story the children will enjoy acting out as you direct them. Have the children start the rhyme standing up.

Mighty, mighty Gideon *(make strong arms)*—
A warrior was he. *(Pretend to hold a shield in front and a sword above your head.)*
Sat down and worried *(sit down),*
Scared as he could be. *(Shake body nervously.)*

One day God told Gideon *(point up to God)*
To be brave and strong. *(Sit up straight and show strong arms.)*
"You'll defeat the Midianites.
Watch me. It won't take long." *(Make thumbs-up sign.)*

But scared ol' Gideon said *(make scared face),*
"I don't know, Lord. *(Shake head side to side with frown.)*

We would lose too many men *(count on fingers)*
If we battled with a sword." *(Pretend to sword fight.)*

"What makes you worry *(tilt head and hold both hands up)*
And not trust in me? *(Shake index finger back and forth.)*
I am God who made power. *(Hold index finger up in the air.)*
Just watch me and see." *(Put both hands over eyes.)*

"I made the fleece *(stroke the back of your hand as if a lamb)*
So dry, but it can be *(make hands stretch out straight)*
Wet, if you want it. *(Wiggle fingers and thumbs together.)*
Just please trust in me!" *(Motion to come.)*

"Take just a few men *(count on fingers)*
To fight the big crowd. *(Hold arms out wide.)*
They can win without fighting *(fold fist up in the air)*
For the sounds will be loud." *(Put hands over ears.)*

"A hero I'll make you. *(Clasp hands together and raise over head to one side and the other.)*
A hero you'll be. *(Continue as above.)*
But only when trusting *(nod head and point up)*
Completely in me." *(Continue as above.)*

Water Exploration Game

Let kids compare the quickness of drinking water the way Gideon's men did. Place a tarp on the floor with bowls of water placed around the inside of the tarp.

Say: **God gave a man named Gideon a very big job to do. He wanted Gideon to save God's people from their enemies. Gideon got a big army ready.** Have all the children stand up. **But God said he had too many men and so God set up a test to find only three hundred men to fight against the enemies.** Show the children the two ways Gideon's men drank the water by lapping it up or scooping it into their hands and drinking it. Give the children one minute to drink the water using both methods. **The men who drank with their hands went to battle with Gideon and God gave them a great victory!**

Believe and Obey

Have a piece of fleece-like fabric, a spray bottle of water, a flashlight, a plastic pitcher, and a trumpet, perhaps fashioned from aluminum foil. Explain to the children that when you give them the thumbs-up sign, they should say, "Gideon, believe and obey!"

God told a man named Gideon to fight against a large army of men who were the enemies of God's people. Gideon was afraid when he heard this. He was the youngest in his family. He didn't know how to fight an army. What did Gideon need to do? Give the thumbs-up sign. Children respond with "Gideon, believe and obey!"

Gideon wanted to be sure God would help him so he asked God to give him a sign. He put a piece of sheep's wool on the ground. Fold the sheep's wool in half. You'll get one side wet and keep the other side dry. Let the children feel the fabric. **Gideon asked God to make the wool wet but keep the ground dry if God was going to be with him.** Put the fabric on the floor and spray it lightly. Let the children feel it. **And God did it. What should Gideon do now?** Give the thumbs-up sign. ("Gideon, believe and obey.")

But Gideon didn't obey yet. He wanted another test. This time he asked God to make the ground wet and the wool dry. Turn the fabric over so the dry half is up, and spray the floor lightly. **God did it! Now what do you think Gideon will do?** Give the thumbs-up sign. ("Gideon, believe and obey!") **And he did! Gideon obeyed all God told him and finally he had three hundred men to fight with him. God gave him a plan to trick their enemy. What should Gideon do about the tricky plan?** Give the thumbs-up sign. ("Gideon, believe and obey!")

This was the trick. Every one of Gideon's men took a torch, an empty clay jar, and a trumpet. Turn on the flashlight, cover it with the plastic pitcher. Hold the trumpet. **They sneaked quietly over to the enemy's camp. They stood all around it, and when Gideon gave the signal, all his men blew their trumpets.** Hold up your pretend trumpet and have the children make trumpet noises. **And smashed their jars.** Have the children clap their hands loudly. Then remove the flashlight from the pitcher. **All this made such a loud noise that the enemy was so scared they ran away. Gideon and his army had won without even fighting. And it was all because** (Give the thumbs-up sign.) **Gideon believed and obeyed.**

Gideon the Hero

Sing this fun song with motions to help children remember the Bible story and know that God will make them little heroes when they obey him. Sing this song to the tune "If You're Happy and You Know It."

It was Gideon who trusted in the Lord. *(Make praying hands.)*
It was Gideon who trusted in the Lord. *(Make praying hands.)*
He took three hundred men. *(Hold up three fingers.)*
And won the battle without a sword. *(Blow a trumpet.)*
It was Gideon who trusted in the Lord. *(Make praying hands.)*

Oh, you can be a mighty hero too. *(Point to someone, then make strong arms.)*
Oh, you can be a mighty hero too. *(Point to someone, then make strong arms.)*
If you listen to the Lord *(put hand behind ear)*
And obey his holy Word *(make an open book with your hands),*
Oh, you can be a mighty hero too. *(Point to someone, then make strong arms.)*

Samson
Judges 13:24–16:31

Samson is probably one of preschoolers' favorite Bible characters. The accounts of his life we see in the Bible show him as a strong and very brave man. Samson doesn't seem to be afraid of anything, even up to his death. His one weakness, we're told, was his love for Delilah. It's important that the children understand that Samson was a mighty man of God *only* when he put God first in his life. It was only after Samson realized this that God forgave him and gave him back his strength to finish the work God had planned.

Samson Chant

The children will enjoy this chant to the same rhythm as the song "The Muffin Man." After each verse, repeat the chorus.

Chorus:
He's goin' after Philistines,
Philistines, Philistines.
He's goin' after Philistines.
God will make him strong.

1. God made Samson very strong
Very strong, very strong.
God made Samson very strong
So he could do what's right.
(Chorus)

2. Samson fought a great big lion,
Great big lion, great big lion.
Samson fought a great big lion,
And he used just his hands.
(Chorus)

3. Delilah wants to end his strength,
End his strength, end his strength.
Delilah wants to end his strength.
Samson told her how.
(Chorus)

4. Samson was sorry he had told,
He had told, he had told.
Samson was sorry he had told.
God gave back his strength.
(Chorus)

Grow a Samson

For this story craft you'll find it helpful to place the children in groups of two to three with a parent or teen group leader. Before class prepare the supplies for each group to have readily accessible. Each child will need: a small bowl, a nylon knee-high sock, one to two cups damp soil, about a tablespoon of grass seeds, a rubber band, a happy felt mouth, and tacky glue. Instruct the group leader to wait for your cue before handing out each craft supply. Give each child a paper bowl.

Say: **Samson was born a long, long time ago. He had a mommy and a daddy who loved God and who loved him very much. Samson liked to eat good food and he grew big and strong.** Have the children use their bowls and pretend to eat. **God was very pleased with him, too.**

Pass out the nylon socks to the children. Have each child place a sock on his or her arm to create a temporary Samson puppet.

Samson's parents made a promise to God that Samson would follow God and never cut his hair. God honored Samson's promise by giving him super strength—more than any man alive. Have the children use their sock puppet to say, "I promise to never cut my hair."

When Samson was older; he fell in love with a woman who didn't love God. In fact, she didn't really even love Samson. She just wanted to find out the secret of his mighty strength. Let's start making our Samson's head by

putting some dirt inside the sock. Take out the container of damp soil. Have children take turns placing the toe of his or her sock inside the bowl and putting about a half-inch of soil into the toe.

All the Philistine men—those were bad men—wanted to know the secret of Samson's strength. But Samson wouldn't tell his secret. They hoped Delilah could get Samson to tell her, then they would know. **Let's put lots of grass seeds in our Samson's head. These seeds will grow long grass like Samson's long hair.** Let each child measure out about a tablespoon of grass seeds and sprinkle them over the moist soil already in the sock.

Delilah would come to Samson and beg him to tell her the secret of his strength. But he wouldn't tell. One day he told her to tie him up with the strongest ropes there were. So she waited until he went to sleep. **Let's put some more dirt in Samson's head while he's sleeping.** Help the children add one to two cups of soil (depending on how big you want Samson's head).

Then the Philistine men tied up Samson real tight with the newest and strongest ropes they could find. Delilah woke him up shouting, "Samson, look out; the Philistines are here to hurt you." Samson woke up and popped the ropes as if they were spaghetti noodles.

One day Samson was so tired of Delilah's silly games and her continuous begging that he gave in. He told her the secret of his strength: If his seven braids were cut off, he could be tied up since he would be as weak as any other man. **Let's tie our Samson head now.** Help each child use the rubber band to tie the bottom of his or her Samson head securely closed.

That night when Samson fell asleep, Delilah called the Philistine men again. This time they brought their knives to shave off his seven long braids. **Now that you've tied your Samson's head with the rubber band, let's cut the extra stocking that's hanging on the bottom.** Use adult-size scissors for this task. Let children each put their fingers in the proper places, then place your hand over theirs, and snip the excess about half an inch from the rubber band. Have the children place their Samson heads in the bowls with the rubber band end down inside the bowl.

Delilah yelled out, "Samson, the Philistines are here to hurt you. Hurry! Wake up!" When Samson woke up, for the first time in his life he struggled and struggled, but he couldn't get away from the Philistines. The Philistine men grabbed him, and hurt his eyes. Poor Samson couldn't see anymore.

Later, Samson was sorry that he didn't obey God and his parents. He was sorry that he let Delilah talk him into telling the secret to his strength. He cried out to God to please give back his strength so he could defeat the mean Philistines. Let's add Samson's mouth, then find out what God let Samson do to the Philistines. Place a strip of tacky glue on the back of the felt mouths, and give them to the children to put on their Samsons.

Well, Samson was blind and couldn't see for the rest of his life, but God forgave Samson because God loved him. And Samson's hair grew long again. The hair on our little Samsons will grow also. God gave Samson back his mighty strength one last time. One day, while the Philistines were all laughing and yelling at Samson, Samson grabbed two pillars that held up the building and pushed them down. The entire building came tumbling down that day and Samson became a hero. Samson learned that it was more important to obey God than to listen to other people who don't love God. Have the children use a spray bottle to water their Samson heads. In about three to four days, they should start seeing "hair" growth. Supervise your children each week as they water and trim Samson's "hair." Remind children that listening and obeying God is more important than choosing to follow a friend that doesn't make good choices.

Something Sweet From Something Strong

Give the children a small plate with animal cookies and a gummy bear on it to represent the lion and Samson. Place a small, quarter-size spot of honey on the plate for the children to taste during the telling of the Bible story. Begin by saying: **One day Samson was walking from his house all the way into town. All of a sudden a huge angry lion came roaring toward him. Use your crackers and gummy bear to show me what you think Samson did.** Let the children show you with their animal crackers and Samson gummy bear.

God had given Samson super strength because Samson's parents had made a promise to God to never cut his hair. As the lion came at Samson, Samson caught it and killed the angry lion with his bare hands. Have the children eat their animal cookies.

Samson continued on to the nearby town where the woman he wanted to marry lived. Have the children walk their Samson gummy bears around their plates.

Some time later as Samson was walking down that same road, he passed the lion's bones off to the side of the road. To his surprise, a family of bees had set up a home inside of the bones and were making honey already. This was a surprise! Samson loved honey, so he scooped some honey into his hand and ate it as he continued his journey. Invite the children to taste the honey on their plates. Have them try dipping one of their animal crackers into the honey.

Say: What does the honey taste like? The honey tastes sweet because the bees make it from the sweet insides of flowers. Samson went along the road to town happily eating his honey. When he got to the town where he was going to get married, thirty Philistine men were chosen to be part of the wedding. Samson decided to play a game with them. He told them that if they could figure out the answer to his riddle, he would get them all some new clothes. He said, "Out of the eater, something to eat; out of the strong, something sweet." Those Philistine men thought and thought but they couldn't tell Samson the right answer. Let's think about the riddle that Samson told them. Ask:

- What is an "eater" that is strong that we talked about in our story?
- What did Samson find in the lion's bones?

A lion eats things and is very strong. Samson found honey inside the lion's bones that was sweet. Go ahead and eat your gummy bear. Allow time for all children to finish their crackers and gummy bears. Now that you're finished with your snack, let's say Samson's riddle again. This time we'll put motions to it.

Out of the eater (hold hands up with fingers spread apart and roar),
Something to eat (cup one hand and pretend to eat with the other hand);
Out of the strong (hold up strong arms),
Something sweet. (Buzz around like bees.)

The Philistine men never did figure out the answer to Samson's riddle by themselves. God blessed Samson with mighty strength as long as he kept the promise to never cut his hair.

Samson's Prayer

Have the children act out an easy drama to remember the story of Samson. Have the children form groups of four or five. One child will be Samson, one will be Delilah, and the others will be lions and then the Philistines.

Say: **God gave Samson great strength.** Have the child who is Samson make a pose showing strong muscles. **God said there were two things Samson could not do—drink wine and cut his hair. Samson was so strong he could kill a lion with his bare hands.** Have the lions roar and roam around. Have Samson tag one of the lions and the lion should lie down. **Samson loved a woman named Delilah. But she was a friend of the Philistines who were the enemies of God's people. Delilah tried to get Samson to tell her why he was so strong.** Have Delilah say "Please, please!" **Samson finally told her if his hair was cut he would not be strong. That was because of the promise his parents made to God not to cut his hair.** Have Delilah pretend to cut Samson's hair and have Samson kneel. **The Philistines captured Samson and made him a prisoner.** Have the children who were lions now be the Philistines and each hold one of Samson's arms. **Samson was sorry he had not kept his promise to God. Let's all say a prayer like Samson might have said.** Have the children repeat each line after you say it.

> **Dear God,**
> **I'm sorry for all I have done.**
> **Big, strong me thought I was great**
> **And ended up losing all of my strength.**
> **So, dear God, forgive me. I'll let you win.**
> **Just let me kill the Philistine men.**
> **Amen.**

Say: **After that Samson was able to defeat a lot of the Philistine men, and become a wonderful hero.**

57

Ruth

Ruth 1–4

The story of Ruth shows a woman who had unconditional, selfless love for her mother-in-law, Naomi. She demonstrated this love by following Naomi back to her own country and providing for her needs.

I'll Follow You Song

The children will enjoy learning of Ruth's dedication and commitment to her mother-in-law. Sing this song to the tune of "My Bonnie Lies Over the Ocean" to learn of Ruth's words to Naomi.

> Wherever you go, I will follow.
> Wherever you stay, I will too.
> Your people will all be my people.
> And your God, I'll worship with you.
> Fo-llow, fo-llow,
> I'll follow wherever you go today.
> Fo-llow, fo-llow,
> I'll follow you and there I'll stay.

Ruth Follows Naomi Game

Remind the children that Ruth showed her love to Naomi by being willing to follow Naomi to another country and to take care of her. Point out that Naomi's other daughter-in-law, Orpah, was not willing to show that kind of unselfish love to Naomi. Play this modified version of Duck, Duck, Goose to help the children remember how Ruth followed Naomi.

Have the children sit in a circle. Choose one child to be Naomi. Naomi will walk around the circle, tapping each child lightly on the head. As "Naomi" taps a child, have him or her say "Orpah." When Naomi taps a child's head and says, "Ruth," that child will get up and run behind Naomi, around the circle. Naomi will take a seat in the empty spot, and the other child becomes the next Naomi. Have the play continue until many or all of the children have had a turn to participate.

Gleaning the Grain

Help the children understand that the law of Moses instructed the farmers to leave in the field the grain that the harvesters missed. This was to allow the poor, the foreigner, the widows, and the fatherless to gather for their needs.

Act out the following simple drama to help the children understand how Ruth provided for her mother-in-law's needs.

Before this activity, scatter "grain" all over the floor. For grain, you could use strips of yellow or brown construction paper, strips of paper bags, popsicle sticks, or paper towel holders. Choose children to play the parts of Naomi, Ruth, Boaz, and harvesters. You may want to do the play more than once to give other children a chance to act.

As the drama begins, "Naomi" and "Ruth" are in a corner of the room. The harvesters are picking up the pieces of grain and putting them in baskets. "Boaz" is watching over the harvesters.

Ruth: *(to Naomi)* I will go get some food.
Naomi: *(to Ruth)* Thank you, my daughter.
(Ruth walks towards Boaz.)
Ruth: *(to Boaz)* My mother-in-law is hungry. May I please gather some grain?
Boaz: Yes, you may. And I will give you extra food for your kindness.
Ruth: Thank you.
(Ruth walks away and begins to gather grain.)

Ruth Marries Boaz Finger Play

The children will enjoy learning that by being faithful to her mother-in-law, Ruth now has a new husband that will provide for both women and that she eventually has a son.

Learn this finger play about Ruth's new family.

Ruth *(hold up one index finger)* **loved her mother-in-law.** *(Hold up the other index finger.)*

She loved her very much. *(Link index fingers.)*

Ruth *(hold up one index finger)* **loved her mother-in-law.** *(Hold up the other index finger.)*

She helped and worked and such. *(Link index fingers.)*

Ruth *(hold up one index finger)* **took care of her mother-in-law.** *(Hold up the other index finger.)*

She gave her food to eat. *(Pretend to eat with fingers.)*

Ruth *(hold up one index finger)* **took care of her mother-in-law.** *(Hold up the other index finger.)*

She gathered all the wheat. *(Pretend to pick up wheat and put it in a basket.)*

Ruth *(hold up one index finger)* **met a man named Boaz** *(hold up the other index finger)*—

A kind and loving man. *(Cross arms across chest.)*

Ruth *(hold up one index finger)* **met a man named Boaz.** *(Hold up the other index finger.)*

It was part of God's good plan. *(Point up.)*

Ruth *(hold up one index finger)* **married Boaz.** *(Hold up the other index finger.)*

She was a happy one. *(Smile and point to mouth with both index fingers.)*

Ruth *(hold up one index finger)* **married Boaz** *(hold up the other index finger)*,

And then they had a son. *(Pretend to cradle a baby in both arms.)*

Ruth's Heart Sandwiches

The children will learn the story of Ruth's sacrificial love while making a tasty treat. You will need a heart-shaped cookie cutter for each pair of children. Set out a plate with four slices of bread, two slices of cheese and two slices of luncheon meat. Give each child his or her own paper plate.

Say: **There was a lady named Ruth who lived in a land far away from God's people. Her husband had died and she lived with her husband's mother, Naomi. She loved Naomi. Take turns with your partner cutting out a heart shape from one slice of your bread to show that Ruth loved Naomi.** Allow children time to complete this.

Naomi's husband had also died. She was glad she had Ruth with her be-cause she loved Ruth. Cut another heart shape from the other piece of bread

you have to show that Naomi loved Ruth. Be sure to share with your partner. Allow time for children to do this.

Naomi wanted to go back to her family in the land of Judah, the land of God's people. Ruth loved Naomi so much that she decided to go with Naomi. Make a heart from the cheese to show that Ruth was willing to leave her country to follow Naomi. Allow children to cut a heart from the cheese.

When they finally reached the land of Judah, Ruth knew she would have to work hard out in the fields to find food to feed both of them. The owner of the fields was a man named Boaz. He saw what a kind and good person Ruth was and he fell in love with her. Cut a heart shape from the meat to show how Boaz loved Ruth. Allow children to cut a heart from the luncheon meat.

Ruth and Boaz got married and had a little baby. Now Naomi had a grandchild. They all made a happy family. Now put all your things together—put the meat and cheese on your bread—to show that Ruth and Boaz and Naomi and the baby were all together in a family now. Let's eat our happy snack together.

Hannah
1 Samuel 1:1–2:21

The story of Hannah shows a woman who had great faith in the Lord and a strong desire to have a child. When God answered her request for a child, she dedicated the child and took him to the temple to live. Her faith was rewarded by additional children to love.

These fun activities will help your children learn about Hannah's strong faith and God's answers to prayer.

Hannah Has a Baby

Have the children form trios to act out the following simple drama. Designate a child in each group to be Hannah, a child to be Eli, and a child to be Elkanah. Then read the story and have the children follow your directions.

Say: **There once was a man named Elkanah and a woman named Hannah. Elkanah loved his wife Hannah. But they had no children and Hannah wanted a baby very badly. Elkanah and Hannah went to the temple to worship.** Have the children portraying Elkanah and Hannah hold hands and skip or jump to the front of the room. **Elkanah and Hannah prayed.** Instruct "Elkanah" to kneel and fold his hands in prayer, and "Hannah" to stand, fold hands in prayer, and move lips as if praying.

Eli, the priest, saw Hannah's great faith as she prayed to the Lord. Hannah told him (have "Hannah" repeat after you), **"I would like to have a baby."** **Then Eli said to Hannah** (have "Eli" repeat after you), **"May God give you what you wish."**

Hannah was very happy. Have "Hannah" jump for joy and clap hands. **She had faith that the Lord would answer her prayer. Elkanah and Hannah went**

back home. Allow "Elkanah" and "Hannah" to hold hands and skip away. **Soon Hannah and Elkanah had a baby boy.** Have "Elkanah" pick up a baby doll or a folded towel and hand it to "Hannah." **Hannah and Elkanah were very happy.** Instruct "Hannah" and "Elkanah" to say together: **"His name is Samuel."**

Hannah's Baby

Children will create a little baby in a bed as they hear the story of how God rewarded Hannah's faith.

Give each child a plate with one cheese slice, two pretzel sticks, one grape, one slice of thinly sliced ham, and a hollowed out oval-shaped dinner roll.

Begin by saying: **The Bible tells us about a wonderful lady who very much wanted a baby. She prayed to God and promised that if God would give her a child, she would let that child serve God in the church. God heard her and gave her a little son. Let's make a little baby to help us remember that Hannah got a little baby.** Help the children each roll up the cheese slice and put the pretzel sticks on each side for arms. Put the grape at the top of the rolled cheese to be the head. **Hannah loved her baby boy and named him Samuel. She took good care of him.** Have each child lay the baby in the bread and cover it with the ham slice. **Hannah kept her promise to God and let Samuel serve God in the church. God let Hannah have many more children. Let's ask God to help us keep our promises the way Hannah did.** Lead the children in prayer and enjoy the snacks together.

Hannah Took Samuel to Church

Help the children learn this game and song to remind them that Hannah kept her promise to give her son to God. Form two groups. Line up the children in two lines, facing each other. Sing the song to the tune of "The Mulberry Bush." For each verse, have the first pair of children join hands and skip or walk around the group. When the verse is over, that pair will go to the end of the line.

A lady named Hannah wanted a child,
Wanted a child,
Wanted a child.
A lady named Hannah wanted a child,
So she prayed to God.

God said, "Yes, you will have a child,
Have a child,
Have a child."
God said, "Yes, you will have a child."
His name was Samuel.

Hannah took Samuel to the church,
To the church,
To the church.
Hannah took Samuel to the church.
She took him to the temple.

Hannah showed how she loved God,
She loved God, she loved God.
Hannah showed how she loved God.
She gave her son to God.

A Lady Named Hannah Echo Rhyme

The children will enjoy echoing the words to the following rhyme about Hannah and her love for Samuel and her love for the Lord. Say the rhyme, line by line, having the children echo each line after you.

There once was a lady named Hannah. *(Curtsy.)*
She wished for a daughter or son. *(Form arms as if holding baby.)*
She wanted to have a baby *(rock arms back and forth)*
For children, she had none. *(Hold hands out with palms up and make a sad face.)*

There once was a lady named Hannah. *(Curtsy.)*
She prayed and asked the Lord *(put hands together in prayer)*
To give her a little baby *(form arms as if holding a baby),*
A baby for a reward. *(Rock arms back and forth.)*

There once was a lady named Hannah. *(Curtsy.)*
Her faith was very strong. *(Put arms up in a strong arms pose.)*
She knew she would have a baby *(fold arms as if holding a baby),*
A babe before very long. *(Rock arms back and forth.)*

There once was a lady named Hannah. *(Curtsy.)*

God gave her a son so dear. *(Fold arms as if holding a baby.)*
She named the baby Samuel. *(Rock arms back and forth.)*
And gave the Lord a cheer. *(Put arms up in the air and cheer.)*

There once was a lady named Hannah. *(Curtsy.)*
Who gave the Lord her praise. *(Raise arms up in praise.)*
She took Samuel to the temple. *(Walk in place.)*
As a gift for God to raise. *(Put arms out as if giving something.)*

There once was a lady named Hannah. *(Curtsy.)*
She gave her son to God above. *(Put arms out as if giving something.)*
God blessed her with other children. *(Fold arms as if holding a baby.)*
Sons and daughters to hold and love. *(Rock arms back and forth.)*

Baby Samuel Craft

The children will enjoy this easy craft. Provide each child with one empty toilet paper roll, one chenille wire cut in half, one white paper circle with a diameter of about two inches, and two white paper parallelograms (the top length should be about two inches and the bottom length should be about three inches). Before the children begin, use a pencil or scissors to poke two holes in the toilet paper roll, directly across from each other, about two inches from the top. These will be the arm holes.

Begin by saying: **There was a lady named Hannah who very much wanted to have a baby. Her arms were empty.** Show children how to insert the chenille wire into the holes for the arms, then fold them forward. **She went to the temple to pray. She made a promise to God that if she had a son, she would give the baby to God to serve him. God answered her prayer and gave her a son. She was very happy, and named the baby Samuel.** Have the children draw a face on the circle and glue it on the top third of the empty roll. **Even though it was very hard to do, after several years Hannah took Samuel to the temple so he could serve God there. She made a very special robe for him each year.** Have the children use markers to decorate the robe (the two parallelogram pieces). Then glue the decorated robe pieces, one on the front and one on the back. Glue only the top, two-inch line, just below the head. **Hannah kept her promises to God. God gave her other children to hold and love. You can keep your promises to God, too, and that's what God wants.**

Samuel

1 Samuel 3:1-11

his aspect of Samuel's life portrays a young, impressionable boy who had spent most of his early years assisting Eli, the temple priest. One night Samuel heard a voice calling him. At first he thought it was Eli, but after three times Eli told Samuel to listen carefully because it was the Lord speaking to him. Preschoolers will be interested to know that even though Samuel was a young boy he did important tasks in the church and could listen to and obey God. These activities will help your young children learn from Samuel's example to keep their ears and hearts tuned in to God's voice.

Sleepy Samuel

This interactive story will help children understand that God called a young boy to serve him and that it is important to listen to God.

Say: **I have a story to tell you about a boy named Samuel, who heard the voice of God. Let's see what good listeners you are. Each time I say the name "Samuel," you are to jump up and say, "Here I am!" and then lie back down again.** To begin, direct children to lie down and pretend they're sleeping.

<u>Samuel</u> (pause while children jump up and lie down) **was a young boy who loved God and did what God asked him to do. <u>Samuel</u>** (pause) **lived at the church with Eli, the minister. One night while he was sleeping, <u>Samuel</u>** (pause) **heard a voice calling his name. He ran to Eli and said, "Here I am." Eli was very sleepy. He yawned and said, "I didn't call you. Go back to sleep." Then <u>Samuel</u>** (pause) **heard a voice calling his name again. He ran to Eli and said, "Here I am." Eli was still very sleepy. He yawned and said, "I didn't call you. Go back to sleep." For the third time, <u>Samuel</u>** (pause) **heard his name. He**

ran to Eli and said, "Here I am." This time Eli realized that God was trying to speak to <u>Samuel</u> (pause). Eli told him to say, "Speak, Lord, I am listening." One more time <u>Samuel</u> (pause) heard a voice calling his name and he said, "Speak, Lord, I am listening." And God told <u>Samuel</u> (pause) many important things. <u>Samuel</u> (pause) did listen to the Lord that night and for the rest of his life.

Where Is Samuel?

Children will enjoy singing this song to the tune of "Twinkle, Twinkle, Little Star." For fun, sing the song three times, getting louder and faster each time. At the end shout: "Samuel! Samuel! Samuel!"

Samuel, Samuel, little boy
Lived with Eli, served with joy.
Late one night his name was said.
Was not Eli, back to bed.
So he listened once again.
Samuel brought God's word to men.
(Shout) **Samuel! Samuel! Samuel!**

Wiggly, Giggly Bugles

The children will enjoy reviewing the story of Samuel being called by God while eating Bugles corn snacks.

Say: **Samuel was a young boy who lived in the temple with an old minister named Eli. Samuel loved God and served in the temple. One night he thought he heard Eli calling him.** Place a Bugles snack in your mouth and call out "Samuel" through the opening. Hand each child a Bugles snack to use to call out Samuel's name. Then allow each child to eat the Bugles snack.

But it wasn't Eli that had called him. Eventually, Samuel and Eli both realized that it was God calling to Samuel. Again, place one Bugles snack in your mouth and call out "Samuel" through the opening. Have each child call out Samuel's name through a second Bugles snack. Allow each child to eat the snack. **This time Samuel answered the Lord by saying, "Speak, for your servant is listening."**

Help children get into pairs and encourage them to call out to each other through their Bugles snacks. They can say meaningful or silly things to each other.

Close this activity by placing a snack in your mouth. Go around to each child and tap him or her on the shoulder. Call out that child's name through the Bugles snack and say: "[Child's name], **be sure to listen to God!**"

Listen, Samuel, Listen

Select one child to be Samuel. Have the child lay down across the classroom on the floor, pretending to sleep, facing away from the other children. Select another child to call out, "Samuel!" Direct "Samuel" to respond with, "Here I am, did you call me?" and see if he or she can guess which child in the group called out. Then select another child to be Samuel and another child to call out Samuel's name. Continue to play until each child has had the opportunity to play the part of Samuel or the caller. If your children are well acquainted with each other, encourage them to call out Samuel's name in a crazy sounding voice.

For variation to this game, have children gather together on the floor. Select one child to go somewhere he or she can't be seen in the room. Help the child reach into a bag of noisemakers, draw one out, make a noise, and then return to the group. Help the group guess what noisemaker made the noise. Continue playing this game until each child has a turn to make the noise.

David
1 Samuel 17

When David fought the giant Goliath, God helped someone little to do something big...and become a hero! This will be a delightful concept for little ones to learn. As preschoolers discover David's faith in God, they will find out that God can help even the littlest people do great things in his name.

David Helps

Lead children in this action rhyme.

David was a shepherd boy with many things to do *(shade hand over eyes and look out over the pasture):*

Protect the sheep, and help his dad, and see his brothers, too. *(Pet the sheep, turn and shake hand with a neighbor.)*

He brought his brothers things to eat, and heard about a man. *(Pretend to eat, then put a hand to your ear.)*

A great big giant who wanted to fight any willing man! *(Stretch and show how big the giant is.)*

The giant named Goliath had called them to a fight. *(Make fists and stand ready to fight.)*

But everyone was too afraid to face him day or night! *(Make a scared face.)*

But David trusted God; he knew exactly what to do. *(Make praying hands, then point upward.)*

So he said, "I will fight him and count on God who is true!" *(Make fists and point upward.)*

With simple stones and lots of faith, David was ready to go! *(Hold out hand, point to stones, cross arms over chest.)*

He attacked the giant and struck him dead, in case you didn't know. *(Twirl a stone to one side and then pretend to let it go.)*

The people were amazed and said, "David, you're first rate!" *(Clap hands and hold up one finger.)*

But David shrugged his shoulders, knowing God was really great! *(Shrug shoulders and point to God.)*

David Trusted God!

Children will enjoy learning about David as they sing this song to the familiar tune of "London Bridge."

David was a shepherd boy, shepherd boy, shepherd boy.
David was a shepherd boy *(put hand out to show the size of a boy)*
Who trusted God! *(Cross arms over chest, then point to God.)*

Goliath was a giant man, giant man, giant man.
Goliath was a giant man *(put hands out to show how tall the giant was)*
Who wanted to fight! *(Put hands on hips and look mean.)*

David took some little stones, little stones, little stones.
David took some little stones, *(Pick up several stones.)*
He trusted God! *(Cross arms over chest, then point to God.)*

David knocked Goliath down, Goliath down, Goliath down.
David knocked Goliath down *(strike chest, then tilt head to the side)*
With God's help! *(Cross arms over chest, then point to God.)*

God Is on David's Side!

Tell this story about David and let the children add movements and sound effects to make it come alive!

David was a shepherd boy who looked after sheep. *(Make sheep sounds.)*
He protected them from lions and bears! *(Make the sounds of lions and bears.)*
His brothers were preparing for a battle, so his father sent David to bring them some food. *(March in place.)*

When David got there, some men told him about a giant man named Goliath who challenged them to a fight. *(Give a big roar, and stand ready to fight.)*

Everyone was too afraid to fight the giant Goliath. *(Chatter teeth and look scared.)*

David said, "I will fight him! I know how to fight lions and bears, and God will be by my side!" *(Make the sounds of lions and bears, then show praying hands.)*

So David took his slingshot and several stones, and went up to face the mean old giant, Goliath. *(Make a loud roar.)*

David swung a stone around his head and it swished through the air and struck the giant Goliath dead! *(Twirl slingshot above head, then make a loud "swish!" sound, then make a loud clap to show that Goliath died.)*

The people shouted, "Hooray for David!" *(Shout "Hooray!")*

David said, "I couldn't lose because God was on my side!" *(Shout, "God was on my side!")*

A Rocky Snack

Have kids help you build this rocky snack as you tell the story of a little boy that did a big job with God's help. Give each child a resealable plastic bag, and three small paper cups. The first cup should contain several vanilla wafers, the second should be half full of grated coconut, and the third should be half full of powdered sugar. You will need thawed orange juice concentrate.

David was the littlest brother in his family who had learned to be very brave while out watching the sheep. One day he had to take food to his big brothers at the place where they were fighting the Philistines. He took bread to them. Put these wafers in your bag to be like the bread David took to his brothers. Allow children to put the wafers in their bags. Have them close the tops and crush the wafers, either by squeezing the bag, or laying the bag down and pushing on the wafers.

But there was problem there. A mean giant man was there and he scared everyone so much, no one would fight him. He had crushed their spirit to fight just like we crushed these wafers.

But God had given David a sweet spirit just like this powdered sugar is sweet. Have children add the powered sugar to the crushed wafers in their bags. David thought about his sheep back home and how God had helped him fight to keep those white, furry sheep safe. This coconut is like the white fluffy fur on the sheep David had back home. Have the children put the coconut flakes into their bags. **David knew God would help him fight the giant. David walked to a little stream.** This juice is wet like the water was wet. Add enough of the juice concentrate into each child's bag to form nonsticky dough. **David picked up stones from the stream to use in his slingshot.**

When David threw the stone, God made the stone fly straight and down came Goliath. We are going to make stones from this dough. Let's thank God for using a young boy to do a big job and ask God to help us do big jobs too. Allow each child to make a small round cookie. Enjoy!

God Helped David

In this finger play, kids will discover that God helped David to do something special! Tell the story and show kids how their fingers can do the talking too!

David was a shepherd boy who tended many sheep. *(Hold up one finger on one hand, and bend the fingers on the other hand.)*

He protected them from lions and bears who tried to kill them! *(Make mean claws with both hands.)*

His brothers were preparing for a battle against the mean Philistines. *(Make mean claws face one another.)*

David traveled a long way and brought his brothers food. *(Walk fingers through the air.)*

David heard there was a giant named Goliath who had challenged them to a fight. *(Place one finger on top of another to show how big the giant was.)*

All the people were afraid, except for David. David knew that if he prayed for God's help, he could fight Goliath. *(Make praying hands.)*

So David walked up to the giant Goliath, taking only his slingshot and stones with him. He swung it over his head and knocked the giant, right on the head! *(Hold one finger much lower than the other and move it close to the taller one. Then crumple the taller finger down.)*

The people were so happy that God helped David fight the giant, Goliath! *(Wave fingers on both hands back and forth.)*

Åbigail
1 Samuel 25

In this story, Abigail showed not only the good judgment that David praised her for, but also incredible resolve and bravery in going out to meet him on the road. In doing so, she saved David from the sins of revenge and murder, and saved her people from destruction at his hands. Use these activities to help your children learn that they can follow Abigail's example of bravery and generosity.

Åbigail's Story

Use this interactive story to tell the story of Abigail. Have children follow your actions and sound effects.

Abigail was married to a man named Nabal. Nabal was very rich, and had lots of sheep. *(Baa like a sheep.)*

David and his men had protected Nabal's sheep in the fields. *(Put hands on hips.)*

Now Nabal was having a party to celebrate all the wool from his sheep. *(Hold belly and pretend to laugh.)*

So David sent his men to ask Nabal for some food. *(Stretch out hands with upturned palms.)*

But Nabal was mean and said "No!" to David's men. *(Fold arms over chest.)*

David's men went back and told David the bad news. *(Shake head sadly.)*

David was angry, and went to attack Nabal. *(Pretend to ride a horse.)*

Abigail heard what had happened, and gathered up lots of food. *(Pretend to pack.)*

She went out to meet David on the road, and asked him to forgive her husband. *(Kneel and clasp hands.)*

She gave David and his men all of the food she had brought, and asked
   David not to sin by hurting her people. *(Stretch out arms.)*
David was happy, and thanked Abigail for helping him not to sin. *(Clap
   hands.)*

Donkey Drive

Before this game, place two baskets filled with equal amounts of paper wads
on one side of the room. Form two groups, and have groups line up across from
the baskets.

Say: **There once was a very rich man who had a wife named Abigail.
David and his men had been protecting Nabal's sheep and they were all very
hungry. Even though Nabal had lots of extra food, he didn't want to share
with David and his men. This made David angry because he wanted to take
good care of his men. They had worked hard taking care of Nabal's sheep.
Abigail heard what happened and so she loaded up her donkeys with lots and
lots of food to take to David and his men. The paper wads in the baskets are
the food she brought.** At your signal, have children in each line take turns running to the basket, removing a paper wad, and placing it in a pile near the front of
the line. When all the children have had a turn, say: **Abigail asked David to forgive her husband for not honoring David. Let's cheer for Abigail for doing
what was right.** Lead kids in a round of applause. **Let's ask Jesus to help us do
what's right just like Abigail.** Lead the children in a short prayer.

Abigail Shares

This is a fun way for the children to remember that Abigail was kind and generous, even in a difficult situation. The children will all shout out the line, "Abigail
knew how to share!" after each verse in the following rhyme.

**Here is a story about Nabal and Abigail, his wife.
He was very rich and they lived the good life.**
(Children shout.) **Abigail knew how to share!**

**David was nearby and protected Nabal's land.
Nabal had a party and it was very grand.**
(Children shout.) **Abigail knew how to share!**

David and his men asked Nabal for some food.
They had worked hard and were never rude.
(*Children shout.*) Abigail knew how to share!

Nabal was mean and said, "No food for you tonight."
That made David angry. He wanted to fight.
(*Children shout.*) Abigail knew how to share!

But Abigail, she wasn't rude.
She packed up lots and lots of food
(*Children shout.*) Abigail knew how to share!

Abigail brought lots for the men to eat.
She saved the day by bringing the treat.
(*Children shout.*) Abigail knew how to share!

Abigail Appetizers

Use this snack to remind children of how generous Abigail was in giving provisions to David and his men. Set out paper plates for each child, plastic knives, one bread slice per child, grape jelly in a squeeze bottle, animal crackers, a bowl of corn flakes, and a bowl of raisins. Have children work in pairs.

Say: **The Bible tells us about all the food that Abigail shared with David and his men. First, the Bible says that she packed two hundred loaves of bread.** Have one child of each pair place a slice of bread on each plate. **Then she took two skins of wine made from grapes. This jelly is also made from grapes.**  Have the other child of each pair spread grape jelly on the bread slices. **Then she took five sheep ready to be cooked. Have the first child place several animal crackers on each bread slice. Then she packed a bushel of grain. These corn flakes are made from corn.** Have the other child add some corn flakes. **And finally, she packed lots and lots of cakes made of raisins and figs.** Have the first child add raisins. **After she had packed up all of the food, she went out to meet David on the road. When she met him, she gave him all of the food she had brought.** Have each child serve a snack to someone else. Before children enjoy their treats, say a prayer thanking God for how generous Abigail was, and asking him to help each child in class be generous too.

She'll Be Coming Round the Mountain

Children will enjoy singing this familiar tune to retell the story of Abigail. Sing the song to the tune of "She'll Be Coming Round the Mountain," and lead children in the actions.

She'll be coming round the mountain when she comes. Here she comes! *(Hand shading eyes.)*

She'll be coming round the mountain when she comes. Here she comes! *(Hand shading eyes.)*

She'll be coming round the mountain. *(Turn in a circle.)*

She'll be coming round the mountain. *(Turn in a circle.)*

She'll be coming round the mountain when she comes. Here she comes! *(Hand shading eyes.)*

She'll be riding on a donkey, when she comes. Heehaw! *(Pretend to ride a donkey.)*

She'll be riding on a donkey, when she comes. Heehaw! *(Pretend to ride a donkey.)*

She'll be riding on a donkey. *(Turn in a circle.)*

She'll be riding on a donkey. *(Turn in a circle.)*

She'll be riding on a donkey, when she comes. Heehaw! *(Pretend to ride a donkey.)*

She'll be bringing lots of goodies when she comes. Yum, yum! *(Rub tummy.)*

She'll be bringing lots of goodies when she comes. Yum, yum! *(Rub tummy.)*

She'll be bringing lots of goodies. *(Turn in a circle.)*

She'll be bringing lots of goodies. *(Turn in a circle.)*

She'll be bringing lots of goodies when she comes. Yum, yum! *(Rub tummy.)*

She'll tell David, "Please don't do wrong. Just be nice!" *(Shake finger.)*

She'll tell David, "Please don't do wrong. Just be nice!" *(Shake finger.)*

She'll tell David, "Please don't do wrong. *(Turn in a circle.)*

She'll tell David, "Please don't do wrong. *(Turn in a circle.)*

She'll tell David, "Please don't do wrong. Just be nice!" *(Shake finger.)*

David listened and was happy. Praise the Lord! *(Give high fives.)*

David listened and was happy. Praise the Lord! *(Give high fives.)*

David listened and was happy. *(Turn in a circle.)*

David listened and was happy. *(Turn in a circle.)*

David listened and was happy. Praise the Lord! *(Give high fives.)*

Nathan
2 Samuel 7:1-17; 12:1-14

Nathan pops in and out of the Old Testament as a wise whisperer. He was King David's personal prophet, speaking for God—words both tough and tender. The children will learn what a prophet is through these louder-than-a-whisper activities.

Sing a Song of Nathan

Lead children in this action song sung to the tune of "Sing a Song of Sixpence."

Nathan was a prophet, a special kind of guy. *(Hands to mouth like a megaphone.)*
Nathan was a prophet and I'll tell you why. *(Hands to mouth.)*
God gave the words to Nathan *(reach up),*
Who gave them to the king. *(Reach out.)*
The king obeyed the words from God. *(Bow.)*
And that is why we sing! *(Hands up.)*

Carrying the Words

In this quick game, the children will learn about the job of Nathan the prophet—to take the words of God to the king. Set out empty tissue boxes, enough for each pair of children to have three. Write these words on note cards. On the first card: "This is" and on the second card: "what the" and on the third card: "Lord says." Tape the cards to the boxes so that each pair has a set saying, "This is what the Lord says." Begin by saying: **God chose Nathan for a special job. Nathan was to take the words of God to the king, so the king could know what God wanted him to do. We are going to play a little game to remember Nathan's**

important job. Have the children each find a partner and have the partners stand across the room from each other. Set the three boxes in front of the first child. **These boxes say "This is what the Lord says." Your partner across the room is the king. You are Nathan. You need to take these words to the king. When you get your words to the king I want both of you to shout out, "Nathan brought the words of the Lord."** Allow the children to carry all three boxes at once to their partner. After they have shouted out the sentence, have them switch roles and do the game again.

Mail Box

The children will deliver God's words like a prophet. Draw a picture of a prophet on the outside of a box. Cut out the mouth. Photocopy page 81 taken from 2 Samuel 7. Cut it into enough pieces for each child in your group to have a piece. Lay an open Bible under the box. As you say the poem, have the children drop the words into the mouth. When they all have finished, pick up the box and show them that the words went from the prophet's mouth into the Bible.

Say: **What is a prophet? I'll tell you.**
He speaks the words God tells him to.
God gave the words to Nathan, the words he did bring.
God gave the words to Nathan who gave them to the king.
The words of God are written in the Bible book.
The prophet's words are written here, just look!

A Sweet and Sad Story

Children will experience the same story Nathan told to King David. Have children work in pairs. To tell this tasty tale, you will need a bag of cotton candy and two paper plates for each pair of children.

Say: **David was a wonderful king, but he made a bad choice and took something that belonged to another man. Nathan the prophet told King David a sweet but sad story to make the king understand that what King David had done was wrong. This is the story: There were two men who were neighbors. One was rich and one was poor.** Set out two paper plates by each pair of children. **The rich man had many, many sheep.** Let the children each pull out some of the cotton candy and put several lumps onto one plate. **The rich man had a whole flock of sheep. But the poor man next door had nothing except one little**

lamb. Have one child from each pair put one ball of cotton candy on the other plate. **He raised it from a baby.** Have the other child add more cotton candy to the lamb to make it grow. **His children loved their little lamb. Let's call the lamb Fluffy.** Let the children name the lamb. **Fluffy nibbled from the children's plates and licked milk from their fingers.** Let Fluffy lick their fingers. **Little Fluffy even slept in their arms.** Let the kids pet her as they make sounds like the sheep "baa." **The children loved Fluffy and Fluffy loved them.**

One day a traveler came to the rich man. He said to the rich man, "I'm hungry. Please cook me a meal of lamb stew."

The rich man said, "You can't have one of *my* sheep." And that rich man with all those sheep went next door. He stole Fluffy and gave it to the traveler. Have children push the plate with Fluffy away. **Of course that was mean. But Nathan used this story to show King David how he had also done wrong.** Let the kids snack on the leftover cotton candy.

The Handiwork of Two Friends

Make two hand puppets for this rhyme. Seal the back of two envelopes and cut across one end. Draw a face on the front of one envelope to look like Nathan and a face on the other to look like King David. Instead of drawing, you may photocopy the faces on page 80, cut them out, and glue them to the front of the envelopes. Have the children sit in two lines facing each other. One side will be "Davids" and the other will be "Nathans." Wiggle the Nathan puppet when you say his name, and have the children on that side jump up and then sit back down. Wiggle the David puppet when you say the word "king," and have the children on the other side jump up and then sit back down. Bring the two puppets together at the word "friend," and have the children find one person in the other line to hug. If you have extra time, the children could make their own puppets to use.

Nathan the prophet, the king's good friend,
Speaking God's word again and again.

Nathan the prophet, the king's good friend,
He wasn't afraid of mighty men.

Nathan the prophet, the king's good friend,
He wouldn't let King David pretend.

Nathan the prophet, the king's good friend,
His words are in the Bible from way back then.

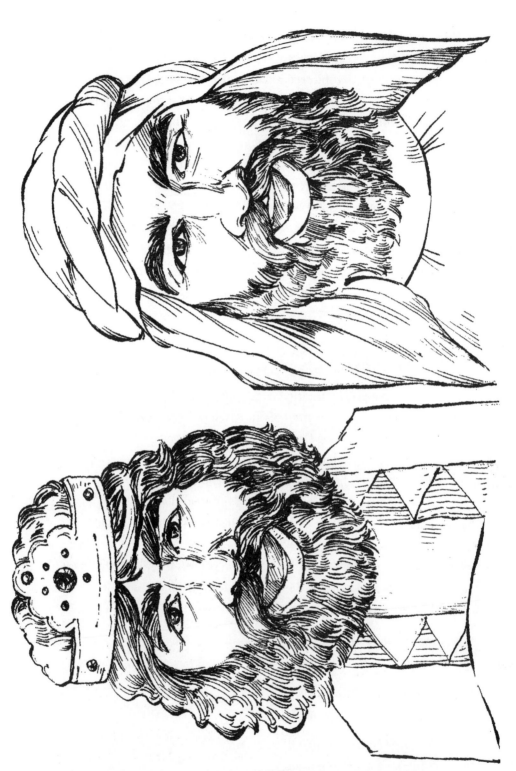

I have been with you wherever you have gone, and I have cut off all your enemies from before you. Now I will make your name great, like the names of the greatest men of the earth. And I will provide a place for my people Israel and will plant them so that they can have a home of their own and no longer be disturbed. Wicked people will not oppress them anymore, as they did at the beginning and have done ever since the time I appointed leaders over my people Israel. I will also give you rest from all your enemies. The Lord declares to you that the Lord himself will establish a house for you.

Solomon

1 Kings 3; 6–7

King Solomon became the most wise man who ever lived and very wealthy. God blessed him because he started his reign with a humble request. Use these activities to teach your children how a humble heart can move the hand of God.

Solomon's Story

Have the children imitate your motions in this action adventure.

Say: **Solomon became the king of Israel.** *(Pretend to put a crown on your head.)*

He wanted to follow the Lord. *(Fold hands in prayer.)*

One night while he was sleeping *(lie down),*

He had a dream. *(Close your eyes.)*

God appeared to him. *(Open surprised eyes.)*

God said, "Solomon, I am pleased with you. *(Fold your hands to your chest and smile.)*

Ask me whatever you want. *(Open your palms.)*

Ask for anything. I will give it to you." *(Open your arms.)*

Solomon sat up. *(Sit up.)*

Wow! Anything? *(Throw your arms wide.)*

King Solomon didn't ask for money. *(Rub your palms together.)*

He didn't ask for horses. *(Trot like a horse.)*

He didn't ask for people to bow down to him. *(Bow.)*

He said, "Lord, I ask you for wisdom *(fold your hands in prayer)*

To be a good king. *(Place your hands on head like putting on a crown.)*

Please help me to know right from wrong. *(Put left palm out, then right palm.)*

God was pleased. *(Happy face.)*

He gave Solomon a wise heart to know right from wrong. *(Put left palm out, then right palm.)*

God also gave Solomon everything he didn't ask for. *(Hands reach out.)*

He gave him horses *(trot),* **gold** *(rub hands together),* **land** *(stomp the ground),* **and people to honor him.** *(Bow down.)*

Solomon became wise, rich, and the most amazing king there ever was! *(Cross arms over chest and then open them up, palms out.)*

Curtsy to the King

Make a simple crown out of paper so that it fits a child's head. The children can help you decorate the crown beforehand with fake jewels. Gather the children into a circle. Choose one child to be King Solomon and let him or her wear the crown. Teach the girls how to curtsy and the boys how to bow when they shout the words "King Solomon." Pass the crown to a different child for each stanza. Repeat so all the kids get a chance to be the king.

Say: **Who was King David's son at birth?**
Who was the wisest man on earth?
(Children shout.) **King Solomon!**

Who built the temple and palace walls?
Who was the smartest king of all?
(Children shout.) **King Solomon!**

Who was the king who knew right from wrong?
Who wrote the Bible books Proverbs and Song of Songs?
(Children shout.) **King Solomon!**

Who had tons of gold, gold, gold?
More than you could ever hold?
(Children shout.) **King Solomon!**

Who had lots of horses and land?
Who did God bless; he became so grand?
(Children shout.) **King Solomon!**

Cartoon on Balloon

You'll complete the face of Solomon on a white nine-inch balloon while the children complete their Solomon faces on paper. Photocopy enough of the "Solomon's Face" handout (p. 86) so each child will have a complete set of facial features. Give each child a sheet of paper with a blank face outline on it, and a glue stick. Set out cut-apart facial features so that all the children can reach them. Make a crown out of the length of a piece of 8½x11-inch paper for each child. The balloon will grow as the story does. After each line, blow the balloon up a little larger, holding it shut with your fingers. Add the underlined facial features to the balloon as the children add features to their paper while you say the poem.

> For King Solomon so wise, let's start by giving him some <u>eyes</u>.
> As his kingdom grows, we'll give him a <u>nose</u>.
> In the meanwhile, here's his <u>smile</u>.
> In a flash, draw a <u>mustache</u>.
> His crown fits now, but not for long. *(Put the crown on him.)*
> When he got old, Solomon did wrong. *(Take the crown off.)*
> Let's give him a <u>beard</u>. It's what I feared!
> His head is growing like his treasure. *(Draw <u>hair</u>.)*
> Soon it will be too big to measure.
> No kingdom on earth lasts forever. *(Put crown on him.)*
> Even for Solomon, rich and clever. *(Release balloon to fly off.)*

Please keep the deflated balloon away from preschoolers! It presents a choking hazard.

Praying Like Solomon

God was so pleased with Solomon's prayer that he gave him even what he didn't ask for! Teach your kids that they can be like Solomon and treasure God's wisdom over material things.

Bring in several toy catalogs or advertisement pages from newspapers (such as department store ads). Ideally, you should have one for every two children. Hand each child some sticky tabs. Say: **God told King Solomon that he would give him whatever he asked for. What would you pick out of this catalog if I could give you anything you asked for? Put a sticky tab on it.**

After they are finished, put away the catalogs. **King Solomon didn't ask for** riches or toys or more crowns or jewels. He didn't ask for a big palace. He asked for wisdom. He asked God to help him know what was right and what was wrong. This made God very happy. He gave King Solomon so much wisdom that he became the most wise man that ever lived. Solomon knew what was right and what was wrong and he shared these secrets with his people and with us in the Bible. Let's say this prayer so that we can please God too. If you have stairs nearby you could have each child say this prayer while walking up a few stairs and then down. Or they could start by squatting down and rise slowly during the prayer. Have each child adapt it according to what he or she picked in the catalog.

Dear Lord,

Please help me to grow up knowing right from wrong. *(Children gradually move up.)*

I want this more than [children fill in the names of the toys they chose.] *(Children gradually move down.)*

Amen.

Kingdom Up, Kingdom Down

Sing this song with the children to the tune of "The Wise Man and the Foolish Man." While the children are singing the first stanza, let them work together to build a tower using cardboard blocks. If you do not have these readily available, use plastic foam bowls, right side up and upside down, to form a palace (a tower). During the second stanza, have the children wag their finger and for the last line, you and the children will figure out what to do!

God told Solomon that he would be the king.
God told Solomon that he would be the king.
God told Solomon that he would be the king.
And King Solomon asked to be wise.

He didn't ask for money, horses, or land.
He didn't ask for money, horses, or land.
He didn't ask for money, horses, or land.
But King Solomon asked to be wise.

So I will pray to always choose right.
So I will pray to always choose right.
So I will pray to always choose right.
So my life will show me wise.

Solomon's Face

Permission to photocopy this handout from *Wiggly, Giggly Bible Stories From the Old Testament* granted for local church use. Copyright © Group Publishing, Inc., P.O. Box 481, Loveland, CO 80539.

The Queen of Sheba
1 Kings 10:1-10, 13

The Queen of Sheba heard of King Solomon's wisdom and his knowledge of the true God of Israel. As the queen of another country, she was brave to travel such a distance, generous to bring such a wealth of gifts, and humble to seek wisdom from another sovereign. Preschoolers can learn to be generous and to seek answers to their questions about God. These activities will help your children learn about the Queen of Sheba and her encounter with Solomon.

What Did She Bring to the King?

Read this story slowly and do the motions with the children. After you have read it once, read it again so the children can do the motions again, as well as remember the story.

On a hot and sunny day *(fan yourself)*
The Queen of Sheba came from far away. *(Point far away.)*
She heard King Solomon was very wise *(Tap your head.)*
And she wanted to see him with her own eyes. *(Point to your eyes.)*

The Queen knew that Solomon was very smart. *(Tap your head.)*
She spoke to him about what was on her heart. *(Place hand over heart.)*
Solomon shared with her the wisdom of God. *(Point to heaven.)*
The Queen was so impressed she began to applaud. *(Clap your hands.)*

She came with her gifts of spices and gold *(hands facing up and out)*
And went home with wisdom that lasted 'til she was old. *(Walk bent over.)*

So, when you have a question, you can ask anything! *(Tilt head to the side and put finger on chin as if puzzled.)*

God will answer—he is our king. *(Hands in prayer position.)*

Camel Caravan

Hand children each a plastic grocery sack and encourage them to stuff their sacks with crumpled newspapers. After they are finished, help children to put the sacks on their backs, like backpacks, with the handles becoming the arm straps. The children now have humps on their backs like camels. Set out two chairs across the room. Choose a child to sit in each of the chairs, one to be the queen and one to be King Solomon. The rest of the children will be the camels that the Queen of Sheba took with her to visit the king. Have the queen stand up and start on her trip to visit Solomon. Have the queen go all over the room, and zigzag back and forth. Direct children to crawl like camels, following wherever the queen goes, eventually to Solomon's throne where she bows. Then choose a new queen and King Solomon and begin again.

King for a Day

Have several small items—toys, game pieces, or pieces of wrapped candy—available for the children. Also provide wrapping paper, scissors, and tape for each child to use to wrap one item. The wrapping will be very sloppy in most cases, but the children will delight in the process. Ask children who would like to be "Wise King Solomon." Seat that child in a chair wearing a crown. Remind children that the Queen of Sheba came with gifts to King Solomon because God had made him wise and she wanted to ask him questions. Tell children to present their gifts to the king and repeat the following rhyme.

Solomon, Solomon, God made you smart.
Here's my gift, for wisdom in *my* heart.

After a few children have presented their gifts, select a new king. Continue exchanging the wise king. If at all possible allow each child to have a gift at the end that they may keep.

The Spice Queen

Before this activity, collect together the ingredients listed on page 90, and a hole punch, tablespoons, one-fourth-cup measuring cups, and one-gallon resealable plastic bags. Photocopy the recipe and the "love note" to attach by folding the handout in half, punching a hole in the upper corner of the handout and in the top of the bag, and tying the handout to each Spice Queen Love Soup ingredient bag. The Queen of Sheba came with gifts of gold, jewels, and spices to share with King Solomon. Tell children you are going to use spices like the Queen of Sheba brought to King Solomon to make a special gift to give away. Set out the ingredients separately around a low table. Pair children so that one is measuring and scooping the ingredients and the other holding the bag. Guide the pairs around the table until each pair has filled two bags.

Spice Queen Love Soup

1 teaspoon each of the following spices:

    thyme, sage, oregano, basil.

Add ¼ cup of the following:

    beef bouillon, minced dry onion, alphabet macaroni,
    yellow peas, lentils, rice, split peas, barley, and
    small shell macaroni.

When you feel you are too busy
and have a meal to fix,

Get a kettle, 2 quarts of water,
1/2-pound of hamburger, and this mix.

Let it cook and simmer
while you have things to do,

But when you sit to eat it, remember:
"I'm thinking of YOU!"

Elijah
1 Kings 18:21-39

Elijah was a prophet who was called upon to make the people decide if they were going to follow the one true God or follow fake gods. He set up a contest to prove which God they should follow. When God sent down fire in answer to Elijah's prayer, the people fell on their faces to worship the one true God.

Preschool children will learn from these activities that it is important to follow Elijah's example and follow the one true God. Your preschool children will learn to respect Elijah as a man who had powerful connections with the one true God.

Elijah's Claim to Flame

Before class, collect a stuffed animal; a plastic toy; a glass food jar with a lid; a small piece of wax paper; a spray bottle of water; some small twigs, rocks, or small blocks like Duplo plastic preschool toys; and matches. Set the wax paper down in the bottom of the jar. For children's safety, make sure they are seated while you do the fire demonstration. Ask the children to sit on the floor near a low table. Sit within reach of the low table and tell children the story of Elijah.

Say: **A long time ago some people followed God and some people followed pretend gods. Sometimes they even followed animals and statues and pretended they were gods.** Pass around the stuffed animal and the plastic toy for the children to see. **Do you think this stuffed animal or this toy can be like God? Can these toys answer our prayers?**

Elijah told the people to follow the real God, not their pretend gods. Back then, people built altars to their gods and shouted and danced to their gods at the altar. Elijah wanted to prove to the people that there was only one true

God and that they should follow him. **So he set up a contest to see if the fake gods or the real God would send down fire to the altars.** On the low table, quickly build an altar with the twigs, rocks, or blocks. Set the stuffed animal on the altar. Tell the children to stand up, jump up and down, and call to the toy to send fire. **Elijah made fun of them and told them to shout louder.** Encourage the children to shout even louder. Clap your hands to get the children's attention back and direct them to be seated. Ask: **Did the pretend god send fire?** Wait for answers.

Elijah was a prophet sent by God to teach people to follow the real God. Elijah even added water to his altar to prove that God could send fire even if the altar was wet. Spray water on the children's hands and then on the altar. **Elijah prayed to God and asked him to send fire. Elijah said, "Hear me, Lord. Show these people that you are the real God. Send your fire!"** Set the jar with the wax paper behind the block altar. Drop a burning match inside. **God sent the fire. The people fell down and called out, "The Lord is the real God!"**

For the children's safety, make sure they are all seated while you tell the last part of the story. As soon as they all see the fire inside the jar, spray some water inside and put the lid on the jar to put the fire out.

"Prophet-able" Power

Have the children form three groups. Tell children you are going to act out the story of Elijah. Give red, orange, and yellow crepe paper streamers to the Flame Dancers. Give large blocks to the Altar Builders. If you don't have blocks, stuff paper grocery sacks with crumpled newspapers and slip another paper sack onto each one to make them. The third group will be the Shouters, Stompers, and Pray-ers.

Direct the Flame Dancers to crouch down into a ball on the floor. Tell them they may only stand up and wave their "fire" streamers when someone prays to the real God. Direct the Altar Builders group to build an altar around the Flame Dancers. Tell the third group they are to yell and stomp on the floor and demand the Flame Dancers to make flames. When nothing happens, have an adult dressed in a robe pretend to be Elijah. He will come to the Shouters, Stompers, and Pray-ers and tell them to pray quietly to the true God for fire. The group will kneel on the ground and "Elijah" will softly say, "God, we know you are the real God, please send your fire so everyone will know that you are the real God!" The Flame Dancers will stand up and do a fire dance and knock over the altar.

Elijah's God Answers Prayer

Direct children to gather in a circle holding hands. Have them move around in a circle as you sing this song to the tune of "The Farmer in the Dell."

The people built an altar, the people built an altar.
Hi-ho, the derry-o, the people built an altar.

They shouted to their gods, they shouted to their gods.
Their gods didn't answer when they shouted to their gods.

Have one of the children be Elijah and go into the center of the circle.

Elijah built an altar, Elijah built an altar. (Have "Elijah" choose two or three children to come to the center of the circle, and kneel down to be a pretend altar.)
Hi-ho, the derry-o, Elijah built an altar.

Elijah prayed to the Lord, Elijah prayed to the Lord.
Hi-ho, the derry-o, Elijah prayed to the Lord.

God sent the fire down, God sent the fire down.
Hi-ho, the derry-o, God sent the fire down.

Direct children to clap and sing.
The Lord, he is God! The Lord, he is God!
Hi-ho, the derry-o, the Lord, he is God!

Awesome Altars

Direct children to gather around a table for this crafty snack. Have the children work in pairs. Give each pair a bowl of peanut butter, plastic knives, a small plate, and small square crackers. The crackers are the building materials and the peanut butter is the "mortar." Direct children to work together to build an altar to the one true God. As they are working, briefly tell about the contest that Elijah set up to prove that the Lord was the only true God. After they have built their altars, sing this song to the tune of "Ten Little Indians."

The prophets prayed but there's no fire.
The prophets sang but there's no fire.
The prophets shouted but there's no fire.
Their god wasn't real.

Elijah prayed and God sent fire.
Elijah prayed and God sent fire.
Elijah prayed and God sent fire.
Our God he is true!

Then celebrate by eating the altars.

Naaman's Servant Girl
2 Kings 5

This book relates the story of a prominent army commander named Naaman, "a valiant soldier" who was highly regarded and had been victorious in battle. In spite of his success, Naaman was doomed because he had leprosy. If it weren't for the faith and belief of his wife's young slave, it's likely that Naaman would have died in agony and alone. However, this slave—a child who had been taken from her homeland—bravely suggested a prophet of God for healing. As a result, the prophet Elisha healed Naaman in the name of God.

Use these activities to help the little ones in your class see what can happen when we share our faith in God, and help them understand that God will do amazing things when we are faithful.

Give the Girl a Hand

Hold out your hand, with your palm up, and have children do the same. Guide them in the simple actions while you tell the story of Naaman's servant girl.

Bend your pinky finger in toward your palm using your other hand.
Naaman sadly lay in his bed.
He had sores on his body—from his feet to his head.
There was no cure, no one could tell
If Naaman, poor Naaman, would ever be well!

Keep your pinky down and bend your thumb in toward your palm.
One little servant girl, she knew the cure!
The man of God could heal Naaman for sure!
"My master should go see Elisha," she did say,
"For only *his* God can make those sores go away!"

Keep the other fingers down and bend your ring finger toward your palm.
The man named Elisha, he loved God.
He told Naaman to do something quite odd!
"In the big River Jordan, dip seven times.
Then your sores will be gone and you'll feel just fine!"

Keep your other fingers down and bend your middle finger toward your palm.
The long, muddy Jordan didn't look very great.
It looked awfully dirty, and Naaman said, "Wait!"
But when Naaman obeyed and dipped down seven times
His skin came out clean—just like yours and mine!

Hold up your index finger, as if to show "number one."
"Now I know there is only one God!" Naaman cried.
For without God's help, he would surely have died!
And all because a little servant girl did tell
That only one true God could make Naaman well.

Banana Bath Time

Give each child a sheet of wax paper, or a small paper plate and half of an unpeeled banana, preferably one with a few brown spots on the peel. Scoop a dollop of chocolate pudding onto the center of each sheet of wax paper. Then say: **Look at your banana. What does the outside look like?** Let children respond, then continue: **Your banana might have some brown spots on it. We're going to hear a story from the Bible about a man who had lots of spots on his skin. The man's name was Naaman and those sores were everywhere! If someone didn't make Naaman well, he would die from those sores. Naaman's wife had a little servant girl who loved God. One day, the little girl said, "Naaman should go talk to the man of God named Elisha. Elisha could make Naaman well." So Naaman went to see Elisha...but Elisha told Naaman to do something very strange.**

Elisha said, "Go to the Jordan River and dip your body seven times. Then you will be well." Naaman didn't want to go to the Jordan River! Look at your chocolate pudding. The water in the Jordan looked sort of like that— muddy and brown. But finally Naaman obeyed. Let's dip our bananas in the pudding seven times and gobble them up.

Help children peel their bananas and slowly count aloud to seven, allowing children to dip and eat their bananas each time you say a number. Then say: **Just like your bananas are all gone, Naaman's sores were all gone! And just as that snack made you feel good, Naaman felt very good! He was glad that the little servant girl had told him to go to Elisha. Now Naaman believed that God was the only true God.**

Naaman, Naaman

Lead children in this action rhyme.

Naaman, Naaman, what will you do? *(Shrug your shoulders.)*
You have sores on your arms, your legs and face, too. *(Touch your arms, legs, and face.)*
You'll never get well unless someone heals you! *(Shake head.)*
Naaman, Naaman, what will you do? *(Shrug your shoulders.)*

Little girl, little girl, what will you say? *(Point to your mouth.)*
Your master, Naaman, is sick and he might stay that way. *(Touch hand to forehead, as if feeling a fever.)*
But you know that God could heal Naaman today! *(Point up.)*
Little girl, little girl, what will you say? *(Point to mouth.)*

Naaman, Naaman, could the girl's words be true? *(Tap head.)*
The man of God—he could heal you! *(Point up.)*
So go to him quickly, there's no time to lose! *(Run in place.)*
Naaman, Naaman, could the girl's words be true? *(Tap head.)*

Elisha, Elisha, what must he do? *(Shrug shoulders.)*
Naaman wanted help, so he came to you. *(Point to another person.)*
You say a dip in the Jordan will make his skin new? *(Hold nose and pretend to dip under water.)*
Elisha, Elisha, what must he do? *(Shrug shoulders.)*

Naaman, Naaman, will you obey? *(Point to someone.)*
The Jordan River is dirty and muddy today. *(Move hands back and forth like the waters of a river.)*
Could that yucky water make your sores go away? *(Rub arms.)*
Naaman, Naaman, will you obey? *(Point to someone.)*

Naaman, Naaman, who will you tell *(Cup hands to mouth.)*

About how Elisha's God made you all well? *(Raise arms.)*

"There's only one God!" you might say with a yell! *(Hold up one finger and point to the sky.)*

Naaman, Naaman, who will you tell? *(Cup hands to mouth.)*

Washed Away

Before this activity, use a permanent marker to draw a simple stick figure on sheets of wax paper. You'll need one sheet of wax paper with the drawing for each child. Set out shallow bowls of water and use food coloring to color the water brown or purple. You'll also need blue napkins or paper towels.

Give each child a drawing and say: **The Bible tells us about a man named Naaman. We'll pretend this is Naaman. Naaman was an important man, but he had a big problem. Naaman had sores all over his body that made him very sick. If someone didn't heal him, the sores would make Naaman die! Use your fingers to put spots of water on Naaman's body.**

Demonstrate how to gently drip water on the figure to make spots. When children have added enough spots, continue: **One person knew how Naaman could be well. Naaman's wife had a little servant girl who loved God. She knew that a man named Elisha could use God's power to heal Naaman. The little girl told Naaman's wife and Naaman's wife told Naaman. Soon Naaman went to see Elisha. Elisha didn't just make Naaman's sores go away. He told Naaman to do something strange.**

"Dip your body in the Jordan River seven times. Then your body will be healed." Naaman didn't want to obey. The Jordan River looked yucky! But he finally obeyed. Let's see what that was like. Pretend these blue napkins are the waters of the Jordan River.

Have children open the napkins and lay them over the pictures. The napkins will absorb the water and make the spots disappear. Say: **Naaman's sores were gone! His skin looked clean and new! Naaman believed that there was only one true God who could do something so powerful! He was glad the little servant girl had helped him.**

Esther

Esther 1–10

The story of Esther gives a clear example of how God can use the most unlikely individuals to do amazing things. When Esther—an orphan and a Jew—is chosen over many beautiful women to be King Xerxes' queen, she is placed in a privileged and precarious position. God used Esther's bravery, faithfulness, and bold actions to save thousands of lives. Use these activities to help children discover how brave Esther took a chance and saved her people.

Esther's Edibles

Before this activity, fill several snack-size resealable plastic bags with flavored cream cheese (strawberry or raspberry looks pretty and tastes much like yogurt) or colored marshmallow creme. Squeeze out excess air, seal the bags, then snip a small hole in the corner of each bag. Set out M&M's candies, raisins, and mini-bagels. Lead children in making this colorful snack while you tell them the story of brave Queen Esther.

Say: **A long time ago, the king wanted to choose a wife.** Let each child choose a mini-bagel. **So he looked all over the kingdom for a beautiful young woman.** Show children how to squeeze the "pastry bags" and spread pretty cream cheese over their bagels.

The king found a beautiful young woman who loved God. Her name was Esther. Let children each add an M&M's candy to represent Esther.

Esther's cousin, Mordecai, watched over her at the palace. He was much older—maybe he was a little bit wrinkled like a raisin! Let children each add a raisin.

One day, Mordecai (add another raisin) **heard that a bad man named**

99

Haman had a wicked plan to hurt God's special people. **Mordecai** (add another raisin) **told Esther** (add another M&M's candy) **about the plan. Even though it was very dangerous to go to the king without him asking first, she told the king.** Have each child add a yellow M&M's candy to represent the king.

The king was angry and stopped the plan right away. Have each child add a red M&M's candy. **Brave Queen Esther saved her people!** Hold up a completed snack. **These colorful treats remind me of Esther's crown. Let's eat our colorful crowns and remember brave Queen Esther!**

Soft Scepters

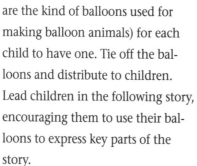

Use a bicycle pump or balloon pump to blow up enough 2-60 balloons (these are the kind of balloons used for making balloon animals) for each child to have one. Tie off the balloons and distribute to children. Lead children in the following story, encouraging them to use their balloons to express key parts of the story.

A long time ago, a king was looking for a special queen. Use the balloon as a telescope and peer around the room. **He found a beautiful woman named Esther and made her his queen.** Touch the ends of the balloon together and hold it on your head, like a crown. **Esther was one of God's special people—she loved God very much. A bad man named Haman didn't like God's people.** Bend the ends of the balloon down to form a frown and hold it in front of your face. **Haman made a mean plan to hurt all of God's people. Esther's cousin, Mordecai, heard about the plan. Mordecai had been like a father to Esther since her parents had died long ago. As quickly as he could, Mordecai went and told Esther.** Use the balloon as a cane as you hurriedly walk. **Esther wasn't supposed to go to the king without being asked, but she was brave and went to the king. She told the king** (hold up the balloon as a scepter) **about Haman's bad plan. The king was angry at Haman and he stopped the plan so God's people were safe.** Wave balloons in celebration. **There was a great celebration for Esther, the brave queen who saved her people!**

> ## Teacher Tip
>
> Although 2-60 balloons are unlikely to pop (unless overinflated), be aware that pieces of popped balloon may represent a choking hazard for young preschoolers. If any balloons do pop, pick up pieces immediately and put them out of children's reach.

Sing It!

Lead children in singing and doing the motions to this song to the tune of "He's Got the Whole World in His Hands." Sing the song several times so children can learn the words.

There's a story in the Bible *(open hands like a book)*
You should know! *(Point to your temple.)*
About a queen named Esther. *(Use hands to make crown on your head.)*
Yes, it's so! *(Nod head.)*
She's from a place called Persia. *(Use thumb to motion over shoulder.)*
Here we go!
Let me tell you what Esther did. *(Cup hand to mouth, as if sharing a secret.)*

A wicked man named Haman *(frown)*—
He was bad. *(Shake head.)*
That wicked man named Haman
Had a plan. *(Tap head and frown.)*
He hoped to hurt God's people
And make them sad. *(Pretend to wipe tears.)*
He thought the king would never know! *(Shake head.)*

Well, good Queen Esther *(use hands to make crown on your head)*
Heard the plan. *(Cup hand to ear.)*
Good Queen Esther *(use hands to make crown on your head)*
Stopped that man! *(Hold out hand to signal "stop.")*
She told the king about it. *(Cup hand to mouth.)*
He was mad! *(Place hands on hips.)*
Esther saved God's people then! *(Raise arms in celebration.)*

Crowning Around

Before class, cut a simple crown from yellow construction paper for each child. Do not tape together the crowns until children are finished decorating them. Set out glue sticks, shakers of glitter, heart-shaped stickers, colorful dot stickers, washable markers, and happy-face stickers.

Set a crown in front of you and say: **The Bible tells us that a long time ago, in a place far from here, there was a king who was looking for a queen. Just like these crowns don't have any pretty jewels on them, the king was missing** a wife. He gathered all the most beautiful women in the kingdom, hoping to find a pretty wife. Show children how to use the glue stick to spread glue over the crown, then shake glitter over the glue. As children follow this step, remind them of all the pretty women in the palace.

From all the pretty women he saw, the king chose a young woman named Esther. Let children each add a heart-shaped sticker to the crown. Esther was not only beautiful, she loved God. Esther was a Jew, which meant that she was one of God's special people. Esther believed in one true God.

The king had a helper named Haman, who was a bad man. Let children add a dot sticker and draw a frown on the sticker. Haman didn't love God's special people. In fact, he wanted to get rid of all the Jews. So he thought up a mean plan.

Esther's cousin, named Mordecai, heard about Haman's wicked plan. Add another dot sticker. Mordecai wanted Esther to tell the king. Esther was afraid the king would be angry, or wouldn't believe her. So she asked all of God's people to pray for her. Add several more dot stickers to represent the Jews who prayed for Esther.

Several days later, Esther went to the king. The king didn't get angry—in fact, he smiled! Let children add a happy-face sticker to their crowns. But when the king heard about Haman's mean plan, he was very angry...at Haman. He got rid of that bad man right away. So, because of brave Queen Esther, God's people were safe. The king even had a party to celebrate what a brave and beautiful queen he had chosen. Tape the ends of each crown together and allow children to wear their crowns while you celebrate brave Queen Esther.

Daniel
Daniel 1–2; 5–6

The story of Daniel, an exiled Jew who became a student in the Babylonian court, shows a young man who was committed to listening to God and being obedient. While in training for the king's service, Daniel obeyed God by refusing to eat certain foods and drink. While in the king's service, Daniel, through visions from God, interpreted the king's dreams and a message that was written on a wall. Daniel also survived being tossed into a lions' den—his punishment for continuing to pray to God, even though the king gave orders not to do so.

From these activities, the children will learn that Daniel listened to God and obeyed him. In turn, the children will learn the importance of listening to and obeying God.

Daniel Eats Healthy Foods

The children will enjoy playing this version of Hot Potato while learning more about Daniel. Seat the children in a circle. Pass a potato around the circle, while chanting the following words. Chant the line first and have the children echo the words. At the end of the chant, the child holding the potato will say, "Daniel ate potatoes and he became strong." Use a different vegetable each time you play the game and change the ending statement accordingly. After you play the game several times, snack on raw or steamed vegetable slices.

Daniel and his friends had to work for the king.
The king wanted them to eat everything.
Daniel said his people could not eat forbidden food.
The ruler thought that Daniel was being very rude.
Daniel said, "Let me eat food that is good for me."

And at the end of ten days, what a difference you'll see."
Daniel and his friends ate the food God okayed.
Daniel was right—what a difference it made!
Daniel and his friends looked healthy and strong.
By obeying God, they couldn't go wrong!

Are You Dreaming?

The children will enjoy learning this song about Daniel's abilities to interpret dreams. Sing the song to the tune of "Frére Jacques."

God gave Daniel
A special job
To see dreams,
And know what they mean.
God gave him the meaning
Of all the king was dreaming.
God gave Daniel
A special job.

After the children have sung the song several times, let them skip around the room while singing to show how happy Daniel was when the king honored him for telling the meaning of the dreams.

Daniel Still Prayed and the Lions Did Roar

Play this creative-movement game to help the children learn about Daniel's ordeal in the lions' den. Choose one child to portray Daniel, one child to be the king, and two children to portray Daniel's enemies. Let the rest of the children pretend to be lions. Start the game with "Daniel" on one side of the room. Direct the two "enemies" to stand on the other side of the room. The "king" can stand somewhere between "Daniel" and his "enemies." Have the rest of the children in the middle of the room, on all fours. Encourage the "lions" to prowl around the room, roar, and smack their lips in hunger as you begin telling the story below. Have the children say the second line in each stanza with you.

Daniel knew how important it was to pray. *(Direct Daniel to get on his knees and pray.)*

Daniel still prayed and the lions did roar.

But there were some men who didn't like Daniel. *(Have the enemies fold their arms on their chests and scowl at Daniel.)*

Daniel still prayed and the lions did roar.

Those men planned a way to get rid of Daniel. *(The enemies should huddle together and whisper.)*

Daniel still prayed and the lions did roar.

Three times a day, Daniel got down on his knees and prayed. *(Daniel should get up and then kneel back down to pray three times.)*

Daniel still prayed and the lions did roar.

The enemies tricked the king with their plan. *(The enemies go to the king and whisper in his ear. Then they return to their side of the room.)*

Daniel still prayed and the lions did roar.

The king said no one could pray to God for thirty days *(have the king shake his finger at everyone)*, but

Daniel still prayed and the lions did roar.

Daniel's enemies told the king that Daniel didn't obey *(the enemies go to the king and point to Daniel)*, but

Daniel still prayed and the lions did roar.

Daniel's enemies threw him in the lions' den *(the enemies move Daniel to the middle of the lions and have him sit down)*, but

Daniel still prayed and the lions did roar.

Daniel's in the lions' den!

Daniel still prayed, but the lions said no more!

Daniel Listened and Obeyed

Help the children learn the following action rhyme to review the events of Daniel's life. Read the story and do the motions, encouraging the children to participate as they learn the repeated verse and motions.

Daniel went to school to work for the king. *(Open hands like a book.)*
He wouldn't eat the food that the man did bring. *(Shake head "no.")*
"That food is not right," said Daniel to the man. *(Point and shake finger.)*
"That food is not part of God's good plan." *(Shake head "no.")*
Daniel ate the food that he knew he should. *(Pretend to eat.)*
Daniel became strong and wise and good. *(Hold arms up to show muscles.)*
Daniel *(form the sign language letter "d" by holding up index finger and touching the other three fingers to the thumb)* listened *(cup hand around ear)* and obeyed. *(Fold hands in prayer and look up.)*

God gave Daniel the ability to see *(use fingers to form circles around eyes like glasses)*
Other people's dreams and know what they mean. *(Rest head on folded hands like a pillow, with eyes closed.)*
The king had dream after dream at night. *(Turn head the other way and rest on folded hands like a pillow, with eyes closed.)*
Those dreams gave the king a terrible fright. *(Open mouth in aghast, with eyes wide open.)*
But God gave Daniel the answer to the dream. *(Point up.)*
And Daniel told the king what his dreams did mean. *(Nod head.)*
Daniel *(form the sign language letter "d" by holding up index finger and touching the other three fingers to the thumb)* listened *(cup hand around ear)* and obeyed. *(Fold hands in prayer and look up.)*

The king had a party with all of his friends. *(Open hands out in front to show many.)*
There were all kinds of food for the women and men. *(Pretend to eat.)*
All of a sudden, a hand did appear. *(Hold up a hand.)*
It wrote on the wall and caused great fear. *(Open mouth in aghast, with eyes wide open.)*
The king had no clue what the words would tell. *(Shrug shoulders.)*
But God told Daniel what the letters did spell. *(Point up.)*
Daniel *(form the sign language letter "d" by holding up index finger and touching the other three fingers to the thumb)* listened *(cup hand around ear)* and obeyed. *(Fold hands in prayer and look up.)*

The king said that no one could worship God or pray. *(Fold hands in prayer and look up.)*
But only Daniel was not afraid. *(Shake head "no.")*

Three times a day, Daniel prayed on his knees. *(Hold up three fingers, fold hands in prayer, and kneel.)*

He was thrown in the lions' den by his enemies. *(Show frightened look on face.)*

Daniel was not afraid of the lions' terrible bite. *(Shake head "no.")*

For Daniel knew that God would keep their mouths shut tight! *(Point up; place hands over mouth.)*

Daniel *(form the sign language letter "d" by holding up index finger and touching the other three fingers to the thumb)* **listened** *(cup hand around ear)* **and obeyed.** *(Fold hands in prayer and look up.)*

Jonah

Jonah 1–4

Jonah didn't just disobey, he did exactly the opposite of what God wanted him to do. He turned his back on God's directions. Preschoolers are old enough to begin understanding that the consequences for disobedience can be very unpleasant. But the real lesson here is the willingness to repent and then obey.

Where Is Jonah?

Lead children in this fun finger play about God's reluctant prophet. Sing the words to the tune of "Frére Jacques."

Where is Jonah? *(Hands behind back.)*
Where is Jonah? *(Hands behind back.)*
Here he is. *(Bring out one thumb.)*
Here he is. *(Bring out the other thumb.)*
God said, "Go to Nineveh." *("Walk" one thumb.)*
God said, "Go to Nineveh." *("Walk" other thumb.)*
Away he ran. *(Put one thumb behind back.)*
Away he ran. *(Put the other thumb behind back.)*

Where is Jonah? *(Hands behind back.)*
Where is Jonah? *(Hands behind back.)*
On a boat. *(Bring out one thumb.)*
On a boat. *(Bring out the other thumb.)*
The sailors threw him overboard. *(Wiggle one thumb.)*
The sailors threw him overboard. *(Wiggle other thumb.)*
Glub, glub, glub. *(Put one thumb behind back.)*
Glub, glub, glub. *(Put other thumb behind back.)*

Where is Jonah? *(Hands behind back.)*

Where is Jonah? *(Hands behind back.)*

In a fish. *(Bring one hand in front and tuck thumb into palm covered by other fingers.)*

In a fish. *(Bring out the other hand in front and tuck thumb into palm covered by other fingers.)*

He asked God to forgive him. *(Fold hands in prayer.)*

He asked God to forgive him. *(Fold hands in prayer.)*

The fish spit him out. *(One thumb behind back.)*

The fish spit him out. *(Other thumb behind back.)*

Where is Jonah? *(Hands behind back.)*

Where is Jonah? *(Hands behind back.)*

In Nineveh. *(Bring out one thumb in front.)*

In Nineveh. *(Bring out the other thumb in front.)*

He did what God had told him. *(Hold up one thumb.)*

He did what God had told him. *(Hold up other thumb.)*

He obeyed. *(One thumb behind back.)*

He obeyed. *(One thumb behind back.)*

Jonah's Big Trip

Have children act out this action rhyme as you teach them the words.

God told Jonah to go and preach. *(Point in the distance.)*
To some evil people God wanted to teach. *(Shake finger.)*

When God said, "Go!" old Jonah said, "No!" *(Shake head.)*
He turned and he ran, and tried to lay low. *(Put arms over head.)*

He hopped on a boat, and began to sleep. *(Pretend to sleep.)*
But a storm came up from out of the deep. *(Make wave motions.)*

The sailors said, "Jonah, God's looking for you!" *(Point finger.)*
So they picked him up and threw him into the blue. *(Pretend to throw something overboard.)*

A big old fish came swimming by. *(Make fish faces.)*
He swallowed Jonah, then said, "Oh, my!" *(Look surprised.)*

Inside that fish, Jonah started to pray. *(Make praying hands.)*
"God, please let me out, and I'll do it your way." *(Nod head.)*

So the fish spit him out right on the beach. *(Make diving motion.)*
And away Jonah went and started to preach. *(Make walking fingers.)*

Fish Food

Treat children to this fishy snack as they learn the story of Jonah.

Set out bread, peanut butter, small round crackers, M&M's candies, teddy bear crackers, paper plates, and plastic knives. Have each child place a slice of bread sideways on a plate. For extra fun, use blue plates to represent water, or let children spread the plates with blue frosting.

Show children how to each cut a triangle from one end of the fish. Say: **This is the mouth of our fish. It helps us think about how God spoke to Jonah and told him to go to a city far away and tell them to follow God's ways.** Have kids spread their bread slices with peanut butter, then attach the triangle with peanut butter as a tail. (Use the illustration as a guide.) **Just like we are putting this part of the bread away from the mouth, Jonah ran away from what God told him to do.** Let children each overlap the small crackers on their bread slices as scales, and add M&M's candy pieces for eyes. Then give children a teddy bear cracker Jonah. **God sent a big fish to swallow Jonah while he was running from God. You can put this Jonah in the fish's mouth. Jonah learned he was wrong not to obey God, and so God had the fish spit Jonah out and he went to the city to talk to the people there.**

Jonah and the Big Fish

Use this familiar game to reinforce the story of Jonah being swallowed by the big fish. If possible, play this game outside or in a large indoor play area.

Choose one child to be the Big Fish. The rest of the children will be Jonahs. Designate a line at one end of your playing area, and have all the "Jonahs" stand behind the line. Designate another line at the other end of the playing area, and call that line Tarshish. Explain to the children that God told Jonah to go to Nineveh, but Jonah did not want to obey God and decided to go to Tarshish instead. Have the "Big Fish" stand midway between the lines. Explain that the object of the game is for the "Jonahs" to try to get to Tarshish without being swallowed (tagged) by the "Big Fish." Have the "Big Fish" call out this rhyme:

> Jonah, Jonah,
> Sailing on the sea.
> You can't get to Tarshish
> Without meeting me!

After this challenge, all the "Jonahs" must leave their line and try to get to Tarshish without being tagged. After each round, players who are tagged join hands with the "Big Fish" and help the children on the ends catch the others. Remind the children that after the fish swallowed Jonah, he was sorry he didn't obey and he decided to obey and go to Nineveh.

Sing-Along Jonah!

This fun song to the tune of "Old MacDonald Had a Farm" is a great active way to explore the story of Jonah. Have the children show thumbs up and thumbs down when they sing those words, and to put hands to ears for the middle verse. Explain that when they do the thumbs-up sign it means a good choice, and thumbs down means a bad choice.

> Jonah, Jonah ran away.
> Thumbs-up? Thumbs-down! No way!
> He ran from God and disobeyed.
> Thumbs-up? Thumbs-down! No way!
> He jumped a ship, took a trip;
> Jonah, Jonah, that's not hip!
> Jonah, Jonah ran away.
> Thumbs-up? Thumbs-down! No way!

> Jonah, Jonah overboard,
> Shoulda listened to the Lord!
> Wrapped up in a seaweed cord,
> Shoulda listened to the Lord!
> Big fish swam up, gulped him down.
> Slimy seaweed all around!
> Jonah, Jonah, overboard,
> Shoulda listened to the Lord!

Jonah, Jonah knelt to pray.
Thumbs-down? Thumbs-up! Hooray!
"God help me out—I will obey."
Thumbs-down? Thumbs-up! Hooray!
With a burp, slurp, whee, and a flee, fly, soar,
Jonah landed on the shore.
Jonah, Jonah knelt to pray.
Thumbs-down? Thumbs-up! Hooray!